ANYONE CAN
PLAYS WI

☆ ☆ ☆

The Absolute Basics of Staging Your Own
At-Home, In-School,
Round-the-Neighborhood Plays

A Smith and Kraus Book
Published by Smith and Kraus, Inc.
One Main Street, PO Box 127, Lyme, NH 03768

First Edition: October 1998
10 9 8 7 6 5 4 3 2

Library of Congress Cataloging-in-Publication Date

McCullough, L. E.
Anyone can produce plays with kids:
the absolute basics of staging your own at-home, in-school,
'round-the-neighborhood plays / by L. E. McCullough. —1st ed.
p.   cm.   — (Young actors series)
Includes bibliographical references.
ISBN 1-57525-151-1
1. Children's plays—Presentation, etc.
2. Theater—Production and direction.
I. Title. II. Series: Young actors series.
PN3157.M37   1998
792'.0226—dc21   98-36282
CIP

ANYONE CAN PRODUCE PLAYS WITH KIDS

The Absolute Basics of Staging Your Own
At-Home, In-School,
Round-the-Neighborhood Plays

by L.E. McCullough

YOUNG ACTORS SERIES

A Smith and Kraus Book

Acknowledgments

☆

Claude McNeal and the cast, crew, and staff of the American Cabaret Theatre; Linda Warder and Diana Gillespie and the Orchard Park Drama Club, Carmel, Indiana; Dr. Kathleen E. George of the University of Pittsburgh Drama Department; folklorists Patrick and Cathy Sky of Chapel Hill, North Carolina; Prof. Sara Reid of the Marian College Music Department; Jeff Waxman and Lisa Asher of Waxtrax Productions; Jim Poyser and Rita Kohn of NUVO Newsweekly; Dr. Sharon Hamilton of Indiana University-Purdue University at Indianapolis; Ray Rice of WISH-TV; Mr. Fred McCashland and Br. John Coakley of Brebeuf Jesuit; Johnny and Marcella Gruelle; my wife Jane; Buddy Lee, Cashondra and The Boy.

Photos by L.E. McCullough featuring the students of Orchard Park Elementary School, Carmel, Indiana.

Dedication

✹

To my granddaughter,
Aubrey Annette Baker aka Aubrey Mouse —
may music and laughter be her friends forever.

Contents

Foreword
WHY PRODUCE PLAYS WITH KIDS?

There are several very good reasons why adults should help kids create and put on plays.

> **Reason #1.** It's a simple, family-centered activity. And it's fun.

> **Reason #2.** It's a potent learning tool for children. And it's fun.

> **Reason #3.** It's a proven method of helping children acquire vital social and communication skills.

Oh, and it's also fun!

Do you detect a pattern here? Playmaking is first and foremost one of the most purely *fun* activities you'll ever enjoy with children. Creating short dramatic works to perform in the house or yard is easy and entertaining. Playmaking inspires kids to learn more about their world. It improves literacy and encourages cooperation and responsibility while stimulating the exercise of imagination. Everyone has to work together to achieve the goal of making the play "happen," thus, everyone's effort is important. Best of all, playmaking allows children to express themselves in positive ways that receive immediate and spontaneous approval from adults and peers alike, which is crucial to nurturing long-lasting self-esteem.

By age four most children have already grasped a lot of the skills necessary for acting; they can memorize, they can mimic, they can dance and sing and easily project themselves into identities outside their own, i.e. "pretend." Even toddlers, if there are older children to guide them, can be incorporated into the action with a "walk-on role" that involves limited speaking.

Playmaking allows parents and children to achieve a "good goal" together. Parents get to see their children at their most vibrant and creative. Children get to excel for their parents, and they become more self-motivated and self-reliant, especially in terms of socializing with other children. By going through the process of creating and interpreting a play for an audience — even if the audience is only the family — parents and children learn to listen to each other better. Playmaking permits families to "act out" their feelings, their problems, their issues in a forthright manner that is nonthreatening because it *is* a play, and as such can be examined from a safe emotional distance. Writing a play about a problem may not resolve the problem, but it does get people talking, and that's the first step toward a solution.

And putting on plays with kids doesn't have to be a hassle. The plays my family and friends performed when I was a child had no costumes or scenery whatever, but our sense of wonder and enjoyment was never diminished one whit. Every playmaking group should exercise maximum creativity toward making the play their own. Preparing for the play is usually as much fun as actually doing it, sometimes more.

Which is why this book has been written: to give you the absolute basics required to stage your own plays at home, school, and in your community — without incurring unreasonable monetary expense or unwarranted blood pressure increase.

Parts One through Seven show the how-to basics of playmaking, from organizing a company and selecting a script to assembling costumes and props, running rehearsals and handling the production's technical aspects. Part Eight translates theory into action by presenting three plays in detail from top to bottom. No matter what ages your kids are, they'll have fun putting their own spin on *Little Orphant Annie, How the People Got Fire,* and *The Story of Silent Night.*

Oh, yes, we were talking about reasons to produce plays with kids. If you're not convinced by the weight of empirical evidence set forth so far, how about this purely selfish motive: Playmaking is the absolute best way you'll ever find to feel like a kid again yourself. And, it's non-fattening.

Now, roll up your sleeves, learn those lines, and break a leg!

L.E. McCullough, Ph.D.
Humanities Theatre Group
Indiana University-Purdue
University at Indianapolis
Indianapolis, Indiana

ANYONE
CAN PRODUCE
PLAYS WITH KIDS

☆ ☆ ☆

Part One
CREATING THE COMPANY

So you're going to put on a play! That is *very* exciting…who are you going to have help you?

Anybody and everybody you can find.

In the professional theatre, producing even a one-person show featuring only *one* onstage actor takes a solid *group* of people working together every step of the way. This group is called the *company*, and the people in the company have very specific titles and very specific jobs that contribute indispensably to the success of the play.

The producer is in charge of making the overall arrangements for presenting the play. In the professional theatre, the producer's chief task is to contribute money, or find other people who will contribute money. For your play, the producer will likely be in charge of mundane but vital tasks such as xeroxing scripts, locating the performance space, running the motor pool, making sure the director and actors and tech crew have the materials and equipment they need.

The director works with the actors and stage crew to interpret the play and bring it from printed page to live performance. The director must not only understand what the play is about but must be able to explain it to the actors. The director is, in essence, a stand-in for the audience during the play's preparation and must have a complete mental overview of everything that is happening onstage. Your director will at times resemble a marvelous combination of Little League coach, choral conductor, camp counselor, handyman carpenter, and master of a three-ring circus. The director is *always* on.

The actors are the individuals who perform the roles designated in the script. In your play, they may double as stage crew members.

The stage crew are the folks who handle the technical aspects of putting on the play, from pulling up the curtain to positioning and operating the stage lights. You'll probably combine a few of these roles to fit the number of volunteers you have on hand to fill them.

- **The stage manager** is in charge of making sure everyone on the stage crew has done their job. During the rehearsal phase, the stage manager collects props and costumes, oversees the construction of sets and scenery, carries out the director's wishes regarding all technical details — lights, sound, set, stage props, etc.

When showtime comes, the stage manager makes sure that props, set, and actors are where they should be before the curtain goes up and lets the actors know when to get into final positions for opening. If the director is not present, the stage manager is often delegated to take the director's place. The stage manager also supervises the "strike," or the dismantling of the set after the final show.

- **The assistant stage manager** helps the stage manager and keeps notes of what goes on during rehearsal, especially any changes in the script. The assistant stage manager often doubles as **the prompter** — the person who stands offstage with a script and helps actors who may have forgotten their lines.

- **The technical director** brings together all the pieces of the set, which may mean building and painting scenery, constructing the stage, gathering furniture, assembling lighting and sound equipment. Naturally, the technical director is aided immeasurably in these tasks by:

- **The lighting director**, who operates the lights and creates lighting effects...

- **The sound director**, who runs the sound system and creates necessary sound effects...

- **The property master**, who maintains all the onstage *properties* (commonly called props) used by the actors or placed around the stage as part of the scenery, from spears and walking canes to tableware and lamps...

- **The costumer**, who assembles (quite often sews) the actors' costumes (clothes, wigs, masks), fitting and dressing them for performance...

- **The dresser**, who helps actors with their costumes before and during the play...

- **The makeup artist**, who may also be the costumer with the added task of helping the actors design, apply and remove makeup, hair dye, face paint, etc.

Are we forgetting anybody? How about **the business team** whose job it is to get the audience to the theatre and make sure they are entertained and well-behaved while inside? Here are some useful people to have in this area:

- **The box office manager** to sell tickets.

- **The program chief** to put together the program, selling ads if desired, and getting the program to the printers and back in time for the performance. The program chief can also make posters and flyers promoting the show.

- **The publicity director** to write up and send out an advance press release about the play to local print and broadcast media. If you were going to place paid advertisements, the publicity director would handle this and also distribute the posters and flyers made up by the program chief.

- **The house manager** to prepare the room for the audience: setting up chairs (and removing them after the show), moving furniture, maintaining appropriate distance between stage and seats.

- **The usher(s)** to assist the house manager in showing the audience to their seats (and pointing out the rest room).

In this book we'll keep things simple, while realizing this may be utterly impossible in Real Life. For instance, the "producer" of your play may be one person or a committee of seven (or six, or five, etc., depending upon work and child-commuting schedules). The "director" may also be the "producer," as well as the "house manager" and the person that flips the lights and cassette player on and off.

In most amateur playmaking, the adults who assume director and/or producer roles will end up shouldering the bulk of organizational responsibility (see the Producer's Handy List of Useful People on the next page). They'll make final decisions regarding *everything*. They'll plan the play, or guide its planning in a collaborative setting with the children. They'll choose the script, hold the auditions, select the cast, decide on the props and set scenery and lead rehearsals. They'll help your volunteer publicity crew get the word out about the show, and they'll let the house manager and stage manager know if the room is set right for performance. And, of course, by opening night, *they* (let's be honest here —*you*) may be the volunteer publicity crew, usher, stage manager, et al.

So, hop to it! Your company awaits!

PRODUCER'S HANDY LIST
OF USEFUL PEOPLE

Keep a tabbed notebook filled with names and numbers of people in these categories. They'll come in very handy the next time you want to do a show and need a quick favor or an impossible task performed yesterday.

Volunteers	Sound Technicians
Lighting Technicians	Stage Managers
Stage Builders/Designers	Stage Setup Crew
Costumers	Makeup Artists
Hardware Stores	Stage Equipment Rental
Musicians	Photographers
Videographers	Flyer Designers
Printers	Publicity Liaisons
Male Performers	Female Performers
Local Youth Performing Groups	Local Theatres
Media Contacts (Print/Broadcast)	

Part Two
CHOOSING A SCRIPT

Here are a few things to keep in mind as you hunt for a suitable script.

No. 1. Your chief consideration is for everyone involved to have fun — adults as well as kids. Thus, for starters, you probably shouldn't try Shakespeare or Molière or O'Neill or Mamet. Rest assured that the kids will learn much of theatrical value from the experience of staging a simple folktale; they don't need to grapple with masters of world drama their first time out.

No. 2. How much time do you have to work on the play? A play of ten or fifteen minutes' duration will give everyone enough to do for a couple weeks; even a five-minute play can be a time-consuming experience in terms of rehearsals, costuming, and scenery building.

No. 3. Remember that *feasibility* — physical and fiscal — are important factors. Can you really do a Siege of Troy in your living room that involves a two-story wooden horse and a cast of a dozen armor-clad warriors? It's also probably not wise to initially attempt plays that require erupting volcanoes, wizards wafting through the air, or even Tarzan swinging from vine to vine in your rose garden. If technology is the dominant element in your play, you'll either end up simplifying and leaving lots to the imagination or ultimately choosing another play without a lot of mechanics and pyrotechnics.

No. 4. How many kids are you planning to have as actors? The answer will tell you how many individual parts your play needs. Try to match the number of kids with the number of parts. If you're considering a play with five speaking parts, but you have ten kids, that means five kids get to be actors and five kids get to be the stage crew. It's possible, of course, to add parts; if you have two royal servants and two extra kids, why not have four royal servants?

On the flip side, if you have five kids and ten individual parts, in most cases you're making a lot of extra work for everybody, and it would be easier to find a play where the individual parts most closely equal the number of available children.

Script Resources

Where do you find a suitable script for your company? You have two choices: Use one that's already published, or create your own.

If you decide to go with an extant work, your local library will likely have several books of children's plays scattered throughout the 792.11, 793.11, 808.2, 808.5, 812, 812.08 sections. These plays can be performed right out of the book with minor adjustments, if you desire, for time and place. Many general bookstores also carry a few children's play collections and can put you in touch with publishers who have more. To get an overview of what's available, check the new *Smith & Kraus Play Index for Young Actors, Grades K–12* by Craig Slaight and Jennifer Esty, an index of 500-plus plays with descriptions and details on ordering the complete script.

Don't forget entirely about copyright. If a play has been written in the twentieth century, its copyright is probably owned by an individual playwright or publishing house. This means you are legally "encouraged" to contact the copyright holder and secure their permission to perform the play. However, if you are not performing the play for commercial use but merely for your own private amusement, this requirement is generally not considered binding. The chances of the FBI showing up at your door because you're putting on a homemade scene from *Cats* for your monthly Brownie meeting is highly unlikely.

Some play books — such as the ones I write for Smith and Kraus — are published so the typical amateur playmaking group can perform them bang off the page without seeking any permission from author or publisher. But if your amateur playmaking group decides to video the play, sell it in Blockbuster stores nationwide and have George C. Wolfe produce it on Broadway, you need to talk to me and my lawyer real quick.

Starting out with a fully realized script has the obvious benefit of lessening your workload as director and producer. You pretty much just have to follow what's written, at least in terms of dialogue, and use your own available resources and imagination as far as costuming, scenery, and blocking.

Some people, however, might want to use their imagination to a greater degree...to an *extreme* degree, in fact. They might want to write their own play!

Writing Your Own Play

If you don't find any plays you like, you can make your own. You can take a literary piece such as a poem, short story, folktale, or chapter from a novel and adapt it for your stage. Or you can dramatize an original idea or story.

Your kids may have a fairy tale they like, or they may want to dramatize a scene from a favorite book. Or maybe a historical event they're learning about in school. Or an incident or legend from the family's history — how Grandpa came to America, the first time Mom took a big trip as a little girl, etc. It's also possible the children may want to dramatize an occurrence in their own lives, such as a family vacation, a school field trip, obtaining a pet, Christmas dinner, and so forth.

If the company wants to do an original play, but the children aren't readily forthcoming with a doable subject, it's time to bring imagination into full swing. The adult can suggest a scenario…walking through the woods, sailing on the ocean, exploring Jupiter, meeting a talking bear at the bus stop…and let the children create characters and plot.

To really plumb the depths of originality, you can focus on remembered emotional states. Have kids think about a time when they were very happy. Or a time when they were very scared. Or very disappointed, lonely, proud, etc. Writing a play based on a "feeling" experience will definitely evoke a strong degree of camaraderie among the children.

And don't forget: The best way to learn to write plays is to read and see lots of plays. That goes for kids, too.

Building the Script

Okay, you've dared to be original and write your own play. Now what?

A play presents a problem that must be solved. The protagonist spends the play trying to solve the problem; the antagonist tries to prevent a solution. That's **conflict**, that's drama.

In its simplest form, the structure of a play has three parts. Part 1 introduces the **protagonist** (usually the hero) and **antagonist** (typically the villain) and other main characters and states the problem that is to be solved. Part 2 heats up the conflict with action that leads to a crisis. Part 3 presents the success or failure of the protagonist to solve the problem — the play's **resolution**.

Part 3 — *climax and resolution*

↑

Part 2 — *conflict builds leading to crisis*

↑

Part 1 — *characters and "problem" introduced*

FIG.1. BASIC PLAY STRUCTURE

Full-length plays often have many problems and solutions that often cause more problems and more possible solutions before everything is resolved at play's end. For a short beginning play with kids, it's best to keep subplots to a minimum. Conflict should appear early. Main characters and their motivations should be clearly drawn. And everything should come to a head — or **climax** — that leads to the protagonist performing some definitive action leading to the resolution.

Keep things simple and practical. When constructing characters and plots, kids can quickly cross the line from inspired imagination to hopeless convolution. Emphasize that every event and every line of dialogue should tell us about the characters and lead to another event further ahead that moves us toward the resolution.

Once subject, plot, and characters have been outlined, you can write some minimal dialogue. Allow children input into shaping the character dialogue according to the way *they* understand them. If this means you have Kennedy and Khrushchev discussing the Cuban missile crisis from the viewpoint of a six-year-old, well, why not? Maybe that's just as sensible as the way it really happened.

Stage Directions

Besides figuring out *what* happens to *who when* and *why*, you need to decide *how* and *where* it all happens. That's what "stage directions" are about.

There are directions that describe time and place (setting).

> *Jenkins' Hardware Store on Main Street, Omaha, Nebraska, 10:02 A.M., Saturday, July 14, 1952.*

There are directions that "set the scene" for the audience, helping them visualize things that are not actually there, such as a mountain, a sunset, a castle pummeled by a raging winter storm.

> *LIGHTS UP STAGE RIGHT AND CENTER ON DINING HALL OF KING WENCESLAS. The King sits on his throne with QUEEN MARTA by his side as FOUR CASTLE REVELERS eat and make merry at the long table. THADDEUS THE PAGE stands to the left of the table, holding a tray, while DUKE BOLESLAV, the King's brother, stands to the right.*

There are directions that tell actors when they enter and leave the stage, where actors are supposed to be on the stage, how they move and how they say their lines with what movement, gesture, and facial expressions.

> At down right JAKE and JENNY assist their AUNT LAURA in the family general store. Aunt Laura stands behind the counter folding a man's work shirt; Jenny stands next to her pouring pinto beans into a container; Jake sits on a stool in front of the counter, writing with chalk on a blackboard slate. TWO COWBOYS enter from left, smiling and carrying saddles in their arms.

There are directions that give information about the characters, their genders, ages, occupations, appearance, mental state.

> JENNIFER is pretty but pouty, fashionably dressed and coiffed in a trendy teen style; she sits on the aisle, frowning and plainly disturbed by the children's ruckus.

Stage Areas

Here is a map of commonly used *stage area* terms. The areas are named from the viewpoint of the actor standing onstage facing the audience.

<u>Back of Stage</u>

UR Upstage Right	UC Upstage Center	UL Upstage Left
CSR Center Stage Right	CS Center Stage	CSL Center Stage Left
DR Downstage Right	DC Downstage Center	DL Downstage Left

<u>Audience</u>

FIG.2. STAGE AREAS

It would be handy for you to learn these terms and make them familiar to your actors and crew as well. They can be shortened, too: downstage left = down left, and so forth.

If you are writing your own play, you can use a variety of script formats. The plays presented in Part Eight are in a standard format you'll find most stage plays published in (see Fig. 3).

DANIEL FERGUSON
What happened to that bandit you were talking to?
ANNIE CHRISTMAS
He took a notion to have a bath. *(sees Bandit #1 coming)*
Looks like we've got more company coming. Gather round...

(She gathers the Fergusons into a huddle, and they whisper together until Bandit #1 enters.)

BANDIT #1
(points to Bandit #3) What happened to him?
SARAH FERGUSON
He fell asleep and dreamed he was in a snowstorm.

FIG.3. STANDARD PLAY SCRIPT FORMAT

Screenplays from movies and television, however, use a slightly different format (Fig. 4).

DANIEL FERGUSON
What happened to that bandit you were talking to?

ANNIE CHRISTMAS
He took a notion to have a bath. *(sees Bandit #1 coming)* Looks like we've got more company coming. Gather round...

She gathers the Fergusons into a huddle, and they whisper together until Bandit #1 enters.

BANDIT #1
(points to Bandit #3) What happened to him?

SARAH FERGUSON
He fell asleep and dreamed he was in a snowstorm.

FIG.4. SCREENPLAY SCRIPT FORMAT

If you have a play mostly composed of dialogue, or don't want to write stage directions into the script, you could use a format like this:

DANIEL FERGUSON: What happened to that bandit you were talking to?
ANNIE CHRISTMAS: He took a notion to have a bath. Looks like we've got more company coming. Gather round...
BANDIT #1: What happened to him?
SARAH FERGUSON: He fell asleep and dreamed he was in a snowstorm.

FIG.5. SIMPLIFIED SCRIPT FORMAT

Whichever format you use, just make sure it can be clearly read and understood by the actors and crew. As well as you! Use this checklist to jot down basic facts about the size and complexity of the production when planning which script to choose.

Play Title _____
Author_____
Copyright Owner/Publisher _____
Performance Playment Terms _____
Performance Venue _____
Anticipated Attendance _____
Number of Acts of Plays _____
Estimated Length of Show _____
Number of Sets _____ Interior _____ Exterior _____
Age Range of Performers _____
Number of Actors _____ Male _____ Female _____
Number of Kids _____ Number of Adults _____
Music Needed _____
Dance Needed _____
Slides/Video Needed_____

FIG.6. SCRIPT SELECTION CHECKLIST.

Part Three
GETTING PREPPED

Your job as director really couldn't be more simple: The children who've chosen to participate in your play are there to have fun; you're going to help them learn how.

Throughout the playmaking process, the director must balance two objectives more or less simultaneously (1) maintain the organization necessary to get the play up; (2) keep things loose enough for everybody to enjoy themselves and want to come back again. You can't put on a play without "structure." But this can be "structure" with a "small s"...a structure of mutual responsibility among company members that supports but does not inhibit the creativity and pleasure playmaking offers.

After a script has been selected, it's time for the director (yes, that would be *you*) to call a full company meeting to make certain everyone is riding the same roller coaster.

First, reaffirm the basic What, When, Where, and Who. Be as specific as possible. "We're going to put on a play for the neighbors who live on our block. We're going to do it in the afternoon this coming July 4th on the big deck in the Weeberschnauzel's backyard."

Second, make sure everyone understands the play's format and how much activity and preparation is required. "This will be a one-act with three different scenes, comprising about ten minutes total. Besides our individual lines, we'll be doing some singing and dancing as a group. We won't have any scenery other than a kitchen table, but we will have costumes and masks that we'll make ourselves."

(...notice the continuous use of first-person plural pronouns...not only an invaluable means of heading off I-me-mine ego disruptions but a gently insistent reinforcement of the idea that working together enhances the fun...)

Third, explain the *company rules*. These are the rules for running rehearsals and company meetings, rules to which everyone must adhere at all times during playmaking. Naturally, the best sets of rules are short and simple. This set has only three.

RULE #1

The director's job is to help us get ready for the play. When the director speaks, we all have to listen very carefully.

There will be many times when you need to stop the whirl of activity and get people refocused. You might find it handy to designate a "freeze" or "reboot" command that, when sounded, brings all activity to an immediate halt: a hand clap, a drum hit, a whistle, a word such as "freeze" or "places." Whatever signal you choose, make certain that kids (and adults) understand they're supposed to stop what they're doing and turn to you with full attention.

RULE #2

When we are in our stage space, we do only things that pertain to the play. If we are not busy doing something in the play, we watch what others are doing.

Most rehearsals will absorb everyone in what's happening onstage. Still, it does no harm to remind everyone that rehearsal is not the place for playing cards or video games, doing homework, braiding hair (unless needed in the play), eating, drinking or making nonessential phone calls. And *never* running or throwing.

RULE #3

We must be ON TIME for every rehearsal and performance. Otherwise, the rest of us cannot do our work preparing the play.

Daily schedule and traffic congestion realities will temper the fastness of this rule. But you likely won't have a lot of time or days devoted to rehearsal in the first place, so it's important to impress upon kids and adults that they make a major effort to be present and ready to get down to business precisely at the designated starting time — just because it makes more time for more fun!

Those are all the Capital R Rules I use. You might lay out additional reminder rules specific to your space — no littering, no riding the family dog, no reprogramming the building's electricity box — that are just basic common sense and good guest behavior.

Here are a few other helpful organizational preliminaries to set forth at your first company meeting:

- Work out a phone tree for contacting parents about changes in rehearsal and performance schedule...and for them to let you know when they won't be able to show up.

- Make sure all kids get a copy of the script, even the ones assigned to tech and publicity work. It helps everyone feel more connected to the play — and you never know when you might need an onstage replacement.

- Create a buddy system among the children in which kids pair up for scriptwork, either in person or on the phone. Assign the buddies the first day of rehearsal.

- Strongly recommend to parents of kids with speaking roles that they find a few minutes each day to help their children rehearse lines with a few simple read-throughs of the script; adult time restraints might make this difficult, but parents will appreciate the opportunity to help when possible.

- Volunteers and other "helpers" are welcome at rehearsals, as long as you can find them specific tasks to assist with. At rehearsals, however, you really don't need an "audience" — i.e., offstage distractions diverting your and the children's attention. Kids and adults who just wander in should be discouraged from doing so unless you can find them something constructive to do.

As director, you'll want to make a *task checklist* for each crew member — most especially yourself. The checklists don't have to be excessively detailed, but they should give everyone an idea of what their job actually entails.

Limbering Up

Even before you select a cast and start formal rehearsals, the director can run a few exercises that get kids eager to work while orienting their energy in a positive direction. These exercises emphasize group participation; even though you'll shortly be breaking the company up into defined roles, it's good for everyone to feel they are part of the company.

Some children may be super shy and reluctant to participate; they need time to come around, which will happen quite rapidly when they see other kids having enormous fun. Don't force participation in group exercises. Simply tell the noninvolved children they can watch but must sit quietly until they feel ready to join in.

Stretching

The company stands in a circle around the director in the center. It's good to incorporate as much visual imagery as you can.

DIRECTOR SPEAKS:

Actors do exercises to get warmed up. We're going to stretch and relax.

Stand up straight with your feet about a foot apart, arms at your sides hanging loosely.

Pretend you're a stork standing by the edge of a beautiful lake...

You're just waking up at the break of day, and you look straight ahead at the sun coming over the water.

It's really beautiful!

Rise up on your toes. Hold your head held high in the air!

Now lower back down, gently and easily like a bird.

Rise up on your toes again.

Now back down, gently.

Lean sideways to your right.

Now lean left.

Stand back up straight, hands at sides.

That's good! You're wide awake and ready to fly!

Here's another exercise.

DIRECTOR SPEAKS:

> *Everybody raise your arms in the air. High as you can!*
> *Reach for the stars!*
>
> *Shake your hands and wave your fingers — keep your*
> *wrists loose.*
>
> *You're reaching so high, you're in the clouds! Feel the*
> *clouds brush your fingers!*
>
> *Rise up on your toes and keep waving your fingers.*
>
> *Back down flat on your feet and lower your arms.*
>
> *Swing your arms at your sides, back and forth.*
>
> *Your arms feel loose, like they're flapping in the wind.*
>
> *Now swing them in front. Your shoulders should feel*
> *very loose.*
>
> *Your elbows should feel very loose.*
>
> *Hands on hips and shout, "Monkey toast!"*

For stretching and relaxing the lower half of the body, have the company lie down on their backs and try the following exercise.

DIRECTOR SPEAKS:

Stretch out full length on your back, arms and hands pointing above your head.

Stretch your legs and feet all the way out and point your toes out as far as they can go.

Bring your toes back toward you.

Point out, pull back...point out, pull back.

Now wag your feet back and forth like windshield wipers — not too fast.

Stop. Lift your right leg up in the air like a big giant crane, then bring it back to the floor.

Lift your left leg up in the air, then bring it back to the floor.

Flex your right knee a few times, kicking out with your toes.

Flex your left knee a few times, kicking out with your toes.

Now sit up and grab your knees and rock back and forth.

Straighten your back and point your shoulders to the sky, hands still holding your knees.

Move your shoulders up and down like a giant bird flying high in the sky.

Relax!

Breathing

DIRECTOR:

> *Here's a simple breathing exercise.*
>
> *Everybody stand up, arms at sides, legs and feet relaxed.*
>
> *Breathe in a big breath, slowly, slowwwwwwly.*
>
> *Hold it...hold it...hold it...*
>
> *Very slowwwwwly, let it out saying "Aaaaah!"*
>
> *Breathe in again, very deep.*
>
> *Hold it...hold it...hold it...*
>
> *Very slowwwwwly, let it out saying "Oooooh!"*
>
> *Now yawn really big!*

Articulation

DIRECTOR:

> *This is an exercise to help us say our lines clearly.*
>
> *Tongue twisters!*
>
> *Start out saying very slowly:*
>
> *How much wood would a woodchuck chuck if a woodchuck could chuck wood?*
>
> *Again!*

How much wood would a woodchuck chuck if a wood-chuck could chuck wood?

Put a tiny bit of space between each word.

How much wood would a woodchuck chuck if a wood-chuck could chuck wood?

Do you hear the rhythm of the words? It's like music, isn't it?

Say it a few more times, starting slowly each time and then slowwwwwly building up speed.

How much wood would a woodchuck chuck if a wood-chuck could chuck wood?

How much wood would a woodchuck chuck if a wood-chuck could chuck wood?

How much wood would a woodchuck chuck if a wood-chuck could chuck wood?

How much wood would a woodchuck chuck if a wood-chuck could chuck wood?

How much wood would a woodchuck chuck if a wood-chuck could chuck wood?

Try this one, slowly:

Sam shaves cedar shingles shiny, soft, and slim.

Again, with space between each word!

Sam shaves cedar shingles shiny, soft, and slim.

Feel the rhythm! Try it again, slowly, then building up.

Sam shaves cedar shingles shiny, soft, and slim.

Sam shaves cedar shingles shiny, soft, and slim.

Sam shaves cedar shingles shiny, soft, and slim.

Sam shaves cedar shingles shiny, soft, and slim.

Sam shaves cedar shingles shiny, soft, and slim.

Vocalizing

DIRECTOR:

This is an exercise to loosen up our vocal cords.

Here is a note. (Hum a note.)

Listen to what I do. I will say five syllables on this one note.

Ma...Me...Mi...Mo...Mu...

These are all long vowel sounds, aren't they?

Listen to me again.

Ma...Me...Mi...Mo...Mu...

Now you try, always staying on this one note.

Your lips and mouth muscles should move and stretch as you say the syllables.

Open your mouth wide! Just like a giant whale swallowing a minivan!

Stre-e-e-e-tch those lips!

Try the vowel sounds again.

Ma...Me...Mi...Mo...Mu...

Good! Now, sing on this note. (Go up a tone and repeat as often as desired.)

This vocal exercise helps loosen your mouth and lip muscles.

Pretend you're very cold and go Brrrrr!

Brrrrr! Brrrrr! Brrrrr!

Let your lips flutter and your cheeks puff out!

Feel your lips vibrate?

It's also similar to when you blow bubbles under water. Brrrrr!

Now, we'll hum these notes, only we'll go Brrrrr! as we hum.

On the next two pages are three simple pitch exercises to enhance flexibility and range. Once you get to the top, start back down again backwards to the bottom!

Vocal Exercise #1

Vocal Exercise #2

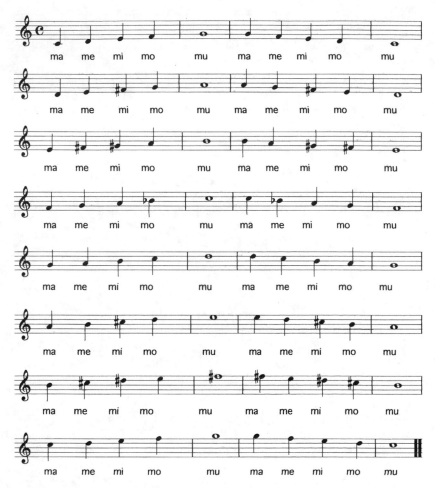

For more vocal exercises greaed to beginning singers, consult the audio cassette *Sing, Anyone Can!* by Marci Lynne. (see Bibliography)

Follow Me, Follow You

DIRECTOR:

Here is an exercise that shows us different ways to move.

One person walks in front of another.

The second person tries to walk exactly like the person in front.

Pair up and let's try it.

First person start walking.

Second person follow behind.

First person walk like a duck!

Walk like a cat!

Walk like a penguin!

Swim like a shark!

Hop like a baboon!

Creep like a mouse on a tightrope!

Walk like your principal!

Walk like your director!

Mirror, Mirror

DIRECTOR:

This is a movement exercise called "Mirror, Mirror."

Pick a partner and face each other standing about a foot apart, arms at your sides.

Choose which of you will be Number One and which will be Number Two.

Every time Number One moves, Number Two tries to match the movement just like in a mirror.

Number One...move your right arm up slowly. Stop.

Number Two move your left arm up.

Number One, turn your head to the left. Stop.

Number Two turn your head to the right.

Number One, bend your knees. Stop.

Number Two, bend your knees.

Try your own movements, Number Ones.

Number Twos try to mirror what your Number One is doing — exactly!

Freeze!

DIRECTOR:

Do you know what a mime does?

A mime tells a story without saying any words.

A mime uses gestures and expressions instead of words, and that's a very important part of acting.

Watch me and see if you can tell what I'm doing.

When someone guesses, I'll stop moving and "freeze!"

(Director holds up both hands as if carefully guiding the steering wheel of a car, honking a horn, mashing down on the accelerator. When someone shouts "Driving a car!," Director freezes.)

Right, I'm driving a car.

Now the person that guessed takes over from me and starts their own mime from my position.

Pass It Around

Here is another mime exercise. Have the company stand in a circle and pretend to pass an object around the circle. Start with something simple like a big, lightweight beach ball. Bounce it, poke it, toss it in the air, outline its shape with your hands, then pass it on to the next person for them to do the same. The idea is for each person to explore the object and its functions using only gestures and facial expressions. Keep progressing to more complex objects — a clarinet, a socket wrench, a tape dispenser, a briefcase.

Puppet Strings

DIRECTOR:

Everyone stand in a circle.

Pretend you're a puppet and stand limp with your head down and shoulders down and knees bent.

Can you feel the strings holding you up?

All of a sudden the puppet master pulls the string attached to your right hand.

Up goes your hand!

Now the string drops and your hand falls back down.

Puppet master pulls the string to your left leg.

Up goes your leg!

Uh-oh, the puppet master is making you dance!

Dance in place as the strings go up and down!

(Director continues to issue commands to the puppets: clap hands, wave good-bye, play a drum, eat soup, etc.)

At the Zoo

One by one, have each person in the circle act out the characteristics of an animal at the zoo — without making the animal's characteristic sounds Everyone else has to guess what the animal is from movements, postures, and facial expressions alone.

The Amazing Incredible Mystery Machine

This is a group exercise that helps kids visualize their actions as part of an onstage whole. First person begins a simple repetitive motion with accompanying sound effect; second person stands adjacent (or above or below) and adds their motion and sound; third person approaches and adds their motion and sound, and so forth until everyone is part of "The Amazing Incredible Mystery Machine."

Say What You Mean, Mean What You Say

DIRECTOR:

> *Good actors are able to use their voices to give special meaning to words.*
>
> *This is called "inflection," emphasizing one word more than other words.*

Let's try to see how many ways we can say a sentence and each time change the <u>meaning</u> of what we're saying by changing the <u>inflection</u>.

First, with no inflection: "Maybe you should feed the dog."

That doesn't tell us much about what's going on, does it?

How about with this inflection: "<u>Maybe</u> you should feed the dog."

What does that mean?

That you could do a lot of things right now, but feeding the dog might get him to stop chewing the carpet.

Then, with this inflection: "Maybe <u>you</u> should feed the dog."

Instead of <u>me</u> feeding the dog!

Or, like this: "Maybe you <u>should</u> feed the dog."

Meaning, you're late for school but you know you'd better put out some food down since you'll be gone all day.

Or, like this: "Maybe you should <u>feed</u> the dog."

Instead of washing the dog! Duh!

And finally, like this: "Maybe you should feed the <u>dog</u>."

And leave the elephant till Mom gets home with fresh peanuts!

Now you think of a sentence you can change with different inflections.

Sunday Comics

DIRECTOR:

Find the comics section of your Sunday newspaper and pick out some age-appropriate strips (with or without dialogue) for the kids to take turns reading and acting out or miming. Strips with animal characters (*Peanuts*, *Garfield*, *Mutts*, etc.) can be especially entertaining!

Monologues

A monologue is a self-contained speech by one character. It may imply dialogue between the speaking character and another unseen or offstage character, but a monologue is essentially one voice, one perspective, one actor. Monologues are excellent exercises for helping actors understand characterization and emotion; they also help prepare kids for the sometimes daunting task of speaking directly to an audience — a skill that will prove very useful in many dramatic situations.

Have the kids write their own short monologues, then memorize and recite them. The monologues can be about occurrences in their daily lives. Here is one called *I Once Was Scared of the Dark*:

I once was scared of the dark. Just about a year ago. When I was five. I was scared 'cause when I went to sleep, I had bad dreams. So I didn't want to go to sleep, and I didn't want to be anywhere in the dark. Alone. Or I would cry. And sometimes throw up.

Then one night I had a bad dream and got scared, and I yelled for my mom. "Mom! Mommmm! Help me, please, the candy cane man is coming to get me! Look out there, the candy cane man is there! Help me, *pleaaaasssssse! Mommmmm!*"

And my mom came, and you know what she did? She took a kleenex and waved it all over my bed. And then she went to my window and opened it up and waved the kleenex around. I said, "Mom, are you wacko?" and she said she was pushing all the bad dreams out the window, and they would never come back. And she flushed the kleenex down the potty and then kissed me good night, and I went to sleep.

And that's how come I'm not scared of the dark anymore. 'Cause I know now that for the rest of my life, even when I get real old, like maybe nineteen or twenty, all I have to do to make bad people go away and not hurt me is take a kleenex and flush them down the potty.

— from *Ice Babies in Oz: 50 Original Character Monologues* by L.E. McCullough. Publisher: Smith & Kraus, 1995.

Now, Relax!

A side benefit of doing these exercises is that you'll get additional insight into your kids' facility for movement, singing, and basic mimicry. This knowledge will come in handy when you face the next task: Assembling the Cast!

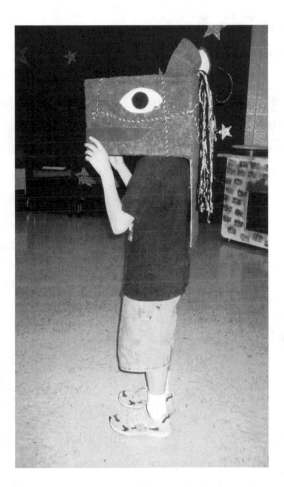

Part Four
ASSEMBLING THE CAST

Natural Talent vs. Growing into the Role

Some kids are natural actors. They make silly faces, goof around, mimic people, extemporize, do television/movie character impressions, and so forth. They can be "on" at the drop of a hat.

Other kids are not so unabashedly outgoing. But they can memorize a part and, with practice and imagination and coaching, "get into" the role.

Matching Kids and Parts

Casting is not an exact science. Even as a first-time director, you'll instinctively realize that the child with a strong, clear voice is best-suited for lead roles that have a lot of words; children with softer voices and less precise articulation can work well with shorter bits of dialogue or in the chorus.

Still, the child you've pegged as shy and undemonstrative in a group setting may turn out — given the chance to step into their individual moment onstage — to be a wonderful actor, opening up and letting loose with real flair.

Most simple plays don't require demanding auditions. The director should gather the company for a first read-through of the script. Get everyone comfortable, sitting in a circle. Have all the children take turns reading and have an adult or two read as well. Don't worry about poor readers, mistakes in pronunciation, or weak vocal projection. These can be worked with and improved.

Instead, look for traits in the child that match the role. Is there a kid that jokes around and giggles incessantly? They'd be great for the role of a scheming trickster or a pompous, obnoxious character who gets a big comeuppance. A child with a more serious demeanor would probably be a solid choice for a grandparent, elderly wizard, king, queen, or other authority figure.

As you read the script a second time, encourage children to put a little "character" into their reading, using voices they think the characters might have.

Helping Children Understand the Play

Before you assign roles, lead a discussion in which the kids talk about the play's theme and characters. It doesn't have to be scholarly or deep, just simple questions from you that help them understand what's happening and why.

Also, take this time to make sure *everyone* knows *all* the vocabulary and pronunciation. That means even (especially) the walk-on spear carrier who has one three-word line. Your play is a learning experience for all, and everyone should be able to have the opportunity to learn new things.

Besides, you never know when the unthinkable might occur to one of the lead actors (chicken pox, flu, broken toe!), and the humble understudy might be required to step into the lead role and save the show.

It can happen in the theatre!

Assigning Roles

Take a short break before announcing the role selections. During the break, the director (in conference with other adults, if desired) should write down the character names on a big notepad and write the names of the selected children next to the assigned role.

Cast Members: "The Story of *Silent Night*"

Fr. Josef Mohr — Tommy
Franz Gruber — Jose
Herr Hummel — Rohan
Frau Schmidt — Melanie
Sexton Sirker — Brittany
Altar Boy — Tanisha
Guitar Student — Shannon

4 CONGREGATION MEMBERS:
• Courtney   • Morgan
• Kerry   • Bobby D.

4 CHOIR MEMBERS:
• Emily   • Bobby M.
• Lindsey   • Amanda

FIG.7. CASTING CHOICE SHEET

Assemble the group again and read the selections. Emphasize that every role is important. If you haven't already done so, create a buddy system whereby kids pair up to help each other with their parts. And remind parents that any few minutes they can spare to help their child learn lines (or simply read through the play) will be greatly appreciated by the company — and the audience!

Before everyone leaves, get the names, phone numbers and addresses of actors, crew, and parents for your play's **contact sheet.** You'll distribute the contact sheet to the company at the first rehearsal. Draw up a reasonably rigid but practical **rehearsal schedule**, emphasizing to everyone that attendance is *vital* and tardiness is a big NO-NO...while realizing that real-world transportation and school schedules will necessitate significant changes as you go along.

How many rehearsals you need will depend on (1) the length and complexity of the play, (2) the age and experience of your actors, (3) how long you have to prepare the play before opening performance, and (4) how many times the entire company can truly meet in full. Go ahead and schedule lots of rehearsals; as you get further into the rehearsal schedule, you'll find cancellations occurring but you'll have a core number of rehearsals to fall back on.

Now, go visit your stage…

Part Five
TECH STUFF

How much time and effort you'll need to spend on the technical aspects of your play depends on the play you've chosen and how realistically you want to present it. If your play is about the Pony Express, you could bring in a real pony, you could build a complete route station, you could have your riders assailed by real snow and sunstroke.

Or you could follow the UYI Rule: Use Your Imagination.

Imagination is at the heart of theatre. Your set, props, costumes, lighting, and sound should *suggest* realism, not replicate it to the last detail. Kids are highly imaginative; even today's computer-nurtured, video-reared young sophisticates will succumb to the spell of the stage and believe themselves to be Indian chiefs in full hue and cry with just a couple feathers stuck in their hair and a streak or two of lipstick daubed on their cheeks.

The technical realm does play a significant part in the theatre, however. Even in a simple production you want objects and effects to enhance and not detract from the presentation. And playmaking can be a great opportunity for parents and kids to share time learning and teaching skills such as sewing, painting, calligraphy, handcrafts, mask making, carpentry, song writing, music composing, and so on.

Children will come up with all kinds of hugely extravagant and fantastic ideas for sets and costumes and props...you, as director/producer will have to exercise judgment on what's practical and what isn't in terms of time, cost, and materials — and, most importantly, in communicating the play's action.

In this chapter, we'll go over some basic technical aspects to keep in mind as you plan your play. Immense numbers of books have been written on each of the technical areas we'll of necessity cover in brief. In my local library I found a book that shows how to make props and scenery from newspapers, another that demonstrates how to fashion costumes without sewing, another that describes how to build sets that stand by themselves, another that offers an in-depth analysis of character makeup. (See booklist page 87.)

There are dozens of such specialized books available in libraries and in bookstores. No matter how simple the technical requirements of your play, go to the library or bookstore and consult them. You'll find a wealth of knowledge ready for immediate use.

The Stage

The **stage** is the space your company will turn into a completely unique world of fun and fantasy. It may in mundane reality be a garage, a driveway, a patio, a church basement, a school classroom, or even just your own living room. But for your play, it will become a castle, a ship deck, a forest, the surface of an alien planet — any place you choose to transport the audience.

You may not have much of a choice in what kind of room you get to make into a stage. But you do need to figure out three basic things. You have to decide where the **acting area** is going to be. This is the actual space in which the actors will be moving while "onstage" during the play.

As you mark out your acting area, you need to consider what your **backstage area** will consist of. This is the "offstage" space in which actors enter and exit from the stage, where costume changes occur, where scenery and props are stored. You'll need at least one and preferably two **entrances** along with some space that is off to the side and out of the audience's sight — the **wings**.

Thirdly, you need to figure out the **audience area**. Where do you want the audience to sit and watch the play?

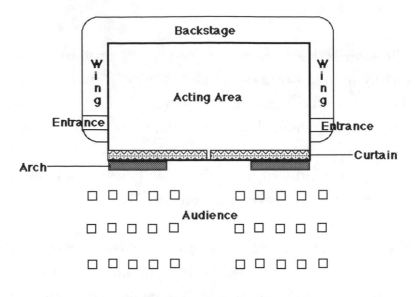

FIG.8. TRADITIONAL PROSCENIUM STAGE

Fig. 8 shows a typical stage space you'll encounter, known as a **proscenium stage**. This is where the audience sits in a single block in front of the stage facing the actors. The division between acting area and audience is very clear. The front of the stage is marked by a curtain and an arch that supports it — this is the actual proscenium. The effect is like that of a picture frame, where the audience "looks in" to the action.

Imagine the stage as a four-walled room — a square or rectangular box. The proscenium is the front of the box, the **"fourth wall,"** so to speak. This is an "imaginary" wall that has been "removed" so that the audience can see what's going on in the room. Some plays pretend this fourth wall is still intact and act as if the audience is nonexistent; others assume the wall is gone and speak and act directly to the audience. We'll talk more in the next chapter about this "fourth wall" concept and how it might affect your presentation.

A second type of stage space is called a **thrust stage** (Fig. 9). This has the audience seated on three sides of the acting area, with a part of the stage called the **apron** extending beyond where the front edge of the stage would normally be.

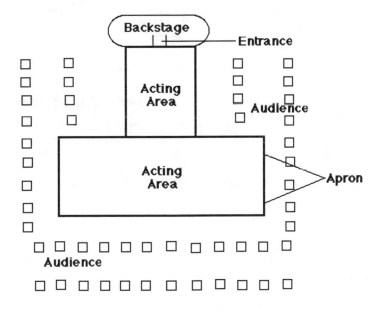

FIG.9. THRUST STAGE

A third stage space is an **arena stage** or **theatre-in-the-round**, where the audience totally encircles the stage (Fig. 10). Obviously, there isn't a curtain or even much scenery on this sort of stage, because that would block the audience's view.

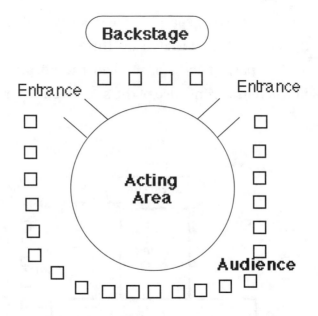

FIG.10. ARENA STAGE

You can also have a **corner stage** (Fig. 11), which makes a more closed-in environment and really gets the audience through the "fourth wall" — and almost into the play itself!

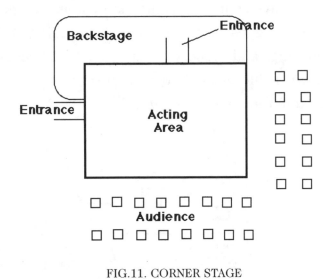

FIG.11. CORNER STAGE

The **wagon stage** (Fig. 12) is literally just that — a stage on wheels than can serve as an instant stage or be moved onto an existing stage or be moved around the room.

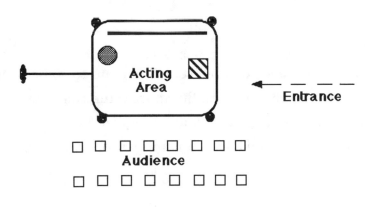

FIG.12. WAGON STAGE

And, if you have some super mechanical and carpentry skills, you can construct a **revolving stage** (Fig. 13), in which the stage and scenery are mounted on a revolving carousel, with different sets (usually just two but possibly more) on different sides of the circle.

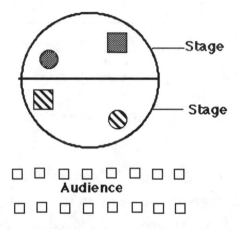

FIG.13. REVOLVING STAGE

The type of stage you choose will depend to some degree on what the play requires. But more often than not, you'll be given an existing stage and be required to work within its confines. Or, you'll have an empty room with four walls, a ceiling, and a floor.

Designing the Stage

Let's say you've got an empty room. You've decided upon a basic traditional proscenium stage. And the acting area needs to encompass 16 feet square. What next?

You need to define your acting area and set it off from the audience. You also have to make sure the audience, especially those in back rows, can see what's happening onstage. Thus, you'll need to raise your stage up off the floor using **platforms** (or **rostra**, as they're called in some theatre books). A platform is a 3-sided box made of a wooden frame and a flat solid top that is nailed, bolted, or screwed into the frame. A platform can be square or rectangular in shape. You can even attach wheels or casters to the bottom and make them mobile.

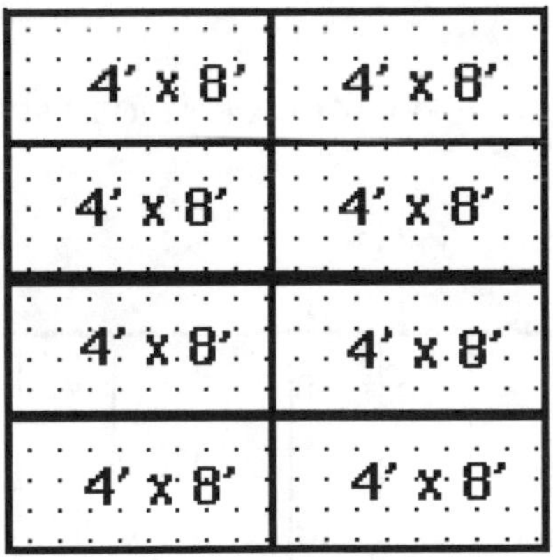

4' x 8'	4' x 8'
4' x 8'	4' x 8'
4' x 8'	4' x 8'
4' x 8'	4' x 8'

FIG.14. A 16' X 16' STAGE
comprised of eight 4' x 8' platforms

Fig. 14 shows a typical stage layout with platforms. Hopefully you'll have one or two semi-experienced handypersons among your volunteers to whip these up.

You'll probably want stationary platforms, with feet or runners at least 4 inches high but probably not higher than 12. Make sure the platforms are solid enough to not wobble or drift apart and to withstand the repeated pounding of exuberant youthful feet; this might necessitate braces underneath the top plank. Always test beforehand whether the platforms can hold the expected wear and tear. Fig. 15 shows a sideview of a platform section; Fig. 16 shows a supporting brace pattern.

top plank is 1" high
outer frame is 5" high

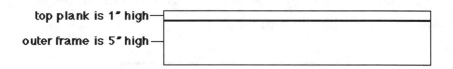

FIG.15. SIDEVIEW OF A PLATFORM SECTION

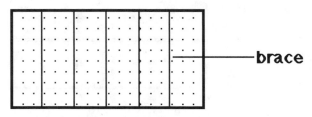

brace

FIG.16. TOPVIEW
showing braces underneath a platform section

For expediting entrances and exits, you might want to attach a **ramp** or two to the stage, or even a set of steps (Fig. 17).

FIG.17. SIDEVIEW OF A PLATFORM RAMP

You can also make your stage **multi-level** and have a ramp that leads up to a box or second platform (Fig. 18).

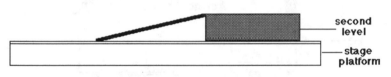

FIG.18. RAMP LEADING TO SECOND LEVEL OF STAGE

Or you can have an entire part of the stage slope upward; this is called a **raked** stage (Fig. 19).

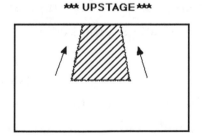

FIG.19. RAKED STAGE RISING TOWARD UPSTAGE

You've undoubtedly heard the expression "waiting in the wings." Well, your stage can have wings for people and things to wait. With a proscenium stage, the **wings** are off-stage areas to the right and left side of the acting area hidden by **flats** or **drapes** that shield actors waiting to come onstage (Fig. 20). Props and scenery waiting to be brought into the play can also be stored in the wings.

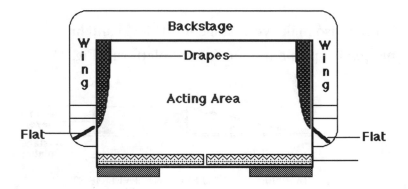

FIG.20. POSITION OF FLATS, DRAPES, AND WINGS

A flat is a platform standing on its end — a very lightweight wood frame covered with canvas that can easily be moved about. The canvas of a flat is usually painted black but can be used to provide a scenic backdrop as well.

Or you might choose to form your wings by simply hanging drapes at the side of the stage. In either case, your wings need to be wide and tall enough to effectively conceal the offstage activity.

As mentioned before, the traditional proscenium stage has a two-part **curtain** at the front that opens in the middle. Your stage, however, may not have this possibility. You may also not have enough offstage area at the sides to have wings. Thus, you must become creative with curtains. If you can't rig them up at the front of the stage, you could put two curtains at the back and have actors enter onstage through the middle (Fig. 21).

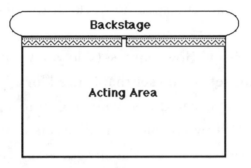

FIG.21. TWO CURTAINS AT BACK OF STAGE
actors enter through middle of opening

Or you could put one curtain up at the back of the stage and have actors enter at the left and right sides (Fig. 22).

FIG.22. ONE CURTAIN AT BACK OF STAGE;
actors enter at right and left of curtain

The Set

"Quiet on the set!"

We've all heard that expression many times, usually with regard to motion pictures and the director's command for silence before an imminent camera "take." In live theatre, **the set** is the space where actors and scenery and props combine to create the specific world of the play.

Your first decision: How many sets do you want? You may employ a **unit set** — one set that is used for all the scenes in the play. Or you can divide your stage into a **permanent set** — a set with two or more smaller sets that represent various separate locations. Usually the stage directions at the beginning of a play indicate the number of sets and their arrangement, but you may choose to use your own creativity.

Next, determine what sort of **scenic features** your set is going to have. Is it an **exterior set** with boulders, waterfalls, mountains, barns, and pyramids? Or is it an **interior set** with tables, chairs, thrones, marble pillars, and fireplaces? Is it a combination of exterior and interior? Are you going to have standing scenery, or are you going to change the scenery every act?

You have several choices for creating scenic features such as backgrounds. The easiest is to simply hang a **drop** or **backcloth** at the rear of the stage from a horizontal pipe, a bar, or a wood strip called a **batten** (Fig. 23). A drop is a piece of canvas or even a sheet that is painted to depict a scene of some kind — inside a room, outside a building, in the sky, under water, whatever you need.

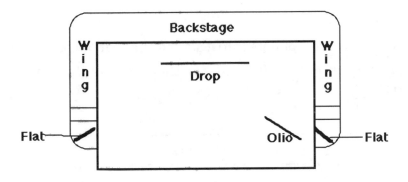

FIG.23. STAGE WITH DROP AND OLIO

An **olio** is a **frontcloth** used at down left or right to hide a costume or scene change (Fig. 23). It can also have scenery painted on it and function like a drop. Drops and olios are typically hung from the ceiling by means of a brace or series of pipes.

If you want something more structural, you can create a **box set** that has tall flats enclosing the stage on three sides (Fig. 24).

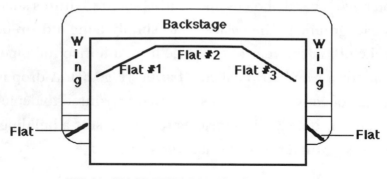

FIG.24. STAGE WITH BOX SET (THREE FLATS)

Or fold a series of flats into a **screen** that can have scenery painted on both sides and switched around if necessary (Fig. 25).

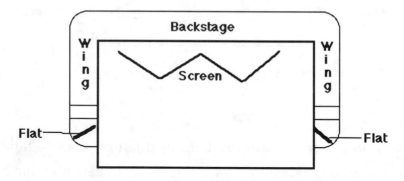

FIG.25. STAGE WITH SCREEN (FOUR FLATS)

You can also make a **cyclorama** — a large curved background piece encircling most of the stage (Fig. 26). Traditionally, cycloramas were painted to suggest the sky, but you can use a white sheet and project slides and light effects for city skylines, rural scenes, or any landscape you wish.

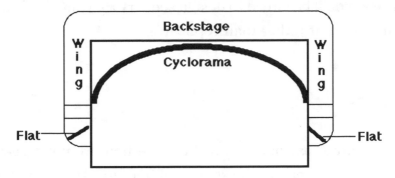

FIG.26. STAGE WITH CYCLORAMA

Related to the cyclorama is the painted **scrim** (or **gauze**) — a transparent, sheer cloth that, when lighted from the front, shows the audience the scene depicted on the scrim; when lighted from the rear, the set (or people) behind the scrim will appear.

Then there are **groundrows** — scenery pieces set low on the ground along the front and sides of stage or in front of drops to suggest things like distant mountains, sea waves, fences, bushes, etc. These can be made out of flats, cardboard, wire, and so on and set to stand with braces at the back. **Cutouts** are larger, taller groundrows that are often rendered as silhouettes.

And you can always build full-fledged **three-dimensional scenery**, if you have the space, time, money. But most often you'll need to keep your scenic features simple and moveable. If you're working with a temporary performing space, you'll be forced to design scenery that "implies" an environment rather than replicates it.

Props

Props are those objects on the stage that are not pieces of scenery or part of the stage architecture. There are **set props** whose function is to define and decorate the stage — tables, chairs, tombstones, campfires, hat racks, etc. Then there are **hand props** — anything that is picked up or carried around the stage by actors during the course of the play, from forks to bazookas to marbles to dog leashes.

You don't need to saturate the set with props; after all, you're not making a movie that requires perfectly realistic physical detail. But a few good props judiciously placed can help denote historic time and geographic location and help define the actors' identities — saving lengthy exposition or dialogue. Props are also sometimes necessary to advance the action and story line.

After you've settled on your stage design and scenery, make a list of the props the play requires (Fig. 27). A Prop List sheet tells you what you need, if you have it yet, where it came from, and if it has been returned after the play. You'll also want to locate a **snatch basket** — a basket or box the stage manager or prop master can use to collect hand props during a scene shift or to store them after rehearsals and performances. Before and during rehearsals and performances, props are often laid out backstage on a **prop table**. Remind the company that props can be touched *only* by people who use them in the play, or by crew members whose job is to maintain them.

PROP LIST

PLAY TITLE: **Greasepaint and Ginthons: The Medicine Show Comes to Town**

Prop Needed	Prop Secured	Source	Returned
3 pound cakes	yes	Mrs. Ward	
cake tray	yes	Mrs. Ward	
harmonica	yes	Joey	
sling shot	yes	Linda	
placard	yes	art room	
easel	yes	art room	
bucket		Mrs. Furillo	
toy six-shooter	yes	Barry	
saddle bag	yes	Leather Shoppe	
a pair of boots (size 10)	yes	Mr. Casey	
Stetson hat (size 7)	yes	Mr. Casey	
long rubber worm	yes	Mr. Foltz	
medicine bottle		Ms. Beck	

FIG.27. PROP LIST

There are many books that supply detailed methods of fashioning props (see Booklist on page 87) out of papier-mâché, polystyrene, plaster, tinfoil, cork, paper bags, egg cartons, cardboard, wood, wire and other basic building and fabricating materials easily purchased at your local hardware store. You'll want to consult these books if you need to create a really unique, one-of-a-kind prop you just can't find in a Goodwill or Salvation Army–type thrift store, or in the basements, garages, attics, and toy closets of your company and volunteers. Treasure Hunt time!

And don't forget, ordinary items like wood crates can be transformed into boulders, thrones, steps, chairs, and so on. They're also easier to pick up and move around than an actual boulder, throne, step, chair, etc.

The stage manager generally oversees the original gathering of the props; the property master takes over prop maintenance during rehearsals and performances. If your company doesn't have a specified prop master, then the stage manager will assume this responsibility and will want to make a Prop Setup List (Fig. 28) that tells what needs to be put out and collected and when.

```
PROP SETUP LIST

Pre-Set:

_____ place 1 chair on top of table
_____ make sure bed is neatly made
_____ place book on desk
_____ give pistol to Gary
_____ put fresh water in glasses on table
_____ place Mary's hat on hatrack


At Intermission:

_____ remove book from desk
_____ give pistol to Mona
_____ remove both chairs from stage
_____ place suitcase behind bed
_____ hang Welcome banner over arch at down left


Post-Show:

_____ throw out water in glasses
_____ take down Welcome banner
_____ collect all hand props and store in prop closet
_____ pick up used pistol caps
_____ help sweep stage and clean up any debris
```

FIG.28. PROP SETUP LIST

Set Plan

Next, figure out a **set plan** — a map that shows where you are going to situate objects on stage, including props. First, sketch out the major set pieces and stage architecture — platforms, furniture, drops, campfires, ramps, and so forth (Fig. 29). Some directors even make scale models of the stage and set, and if you think this would be helpful, go right ahead. It might help you "see" the space better when you begin to plan how to block the actors.

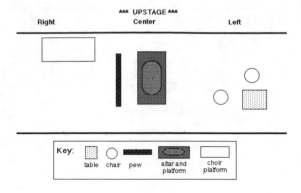

FIG.29. SET PLAN
showing major set pieces and scenery

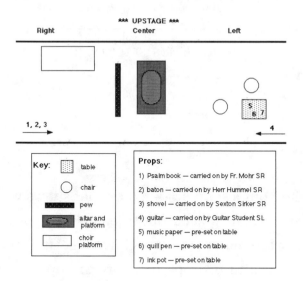

FIG.30. SET PLAN
showing major set pieces, scenery, and props.
SR (stage right) and SL (stage left) indicate which side of the
stage the prop should be placed so the actor can carry it on.

Then, put your props into the picture (Fig. 30), listing which ones are carried onstage by actors and which need to be pre-set onstage before the curtain rises.

Costumes

For a typical children's play on a restricted budget, you're really talking about "symbolic costumes" — one or two or five at most items that signify a character's basic identity. A king, queen, or other royal personage can be capably depicted with a simple crown, a scepter, and a robe or cape with a snazzy bit of trim.

The dedicated children's play costumer will become a constant and obsessive collector of all kinds of clothing and fabric remnants: discarded clothes, towels, blankets, ties, and terminally worn pajamas, sweaters, sweatshirts, gloves, hats, headbands, belts, leotards, socks, wigs — not to mention a plethora of accessories: beads, junk jewelry, eyeglasses, buckles, scarves…and sandals and slippers for just about any play taking place up to 1700 A.D.

A costumer's basic tools include: garment measuring tape, straight ruler, waterproof marking pen, cutting knife, sewing machine, glue, dye, paint, scissors, newspaper for pattern-marking, wire hangers and vast quantities of pins, needles, thread, zippers, buttons, ribbons, rope, string, clasps, braid loops, sequins, elastic, lace, tape, and velcro.

An able costumer quickly becomes a master of sartorial improvisation — learning that plastic trash can lids make excellent shields, shower curtain rings convert into medieval belts, tinfoil shapes neatly into crowns, paper bags provide endless fodder for masks, beards, and feathers, any old blanket can become a dashing cape and a dextrous combination of pipe cleaners, black wool, and soda straws will create a passable Egyptian headdress.

A credible wizard outfit can be constructed from black felt, poster board, glue, some gold or silver vinyl stars and glitter, white crepe for beard and flowing locks. Angel halos can be fashioned from aluminum wire bent into a hoop, connected with duct tape and covered with glitter. Fake fur, dark sweat pants, black vinyl cuffs augment a Viking tunic.

If you're seeking a high degree of historical accuracy, your costumer may want to begin by making sketches of the costumes and consulting period artwork. It's a good idea to have a **costume chart** for each character that tells exactly what clothing and accessories are needed (Fig. 31).

```
┌─────────────────────────────────────────────────┐
│  COSTUME CHART                                  │
│                                                 │
│  PLAY TITLE: The Twelve Months                  │
│  CHARACTER: Dobrunka                            │
│  COSTUME PIECES: Skirt (two inches above shoes) │
│                  Blouse (peasant-style)         │
│                  Stockings (brown)              │
│                  Shoes (with silver buckles)    │
│                  Bonnet (blue)                  │
│                  Shawl (black, fringed)         │
│                  Brooch                         │
└─────────────────────────────────────────────────┘
```

FIG.31. COSTUME CHART

Color coordination is another element that can be important in some plays — you might want everyone in the royal infantry to wear the same color tunic or have the warring Greeks and the Trojans attired in distinctive, clashing hues that make it easy for the audience to tell the warring factions apart.

Always remember that the costume must allow the actor freedom of movement — even if the character is *supposed* to be clumsy.

Makeup

As director, you may find that most of your actors do not need extensive facial makeup to convey their character. However, if you want your Methusaleh to exhibit every single one of his nine hundred-plus years, a bit of cleverly applied paint and powder can help transform a beardless preteen into a wrinkled, hoary old man.

Besides age alterations, makeup is used in the professional theatre to counteract the color-diluting effect of intense stage lighting on actors' faces. It is also used to accentuate certain features that denote a particular type of character (clowns, villains, witches, hobos, hollow-cheeked urchins) or a well-known historical figure — any self-respecting Civil War–era Abraham Lincoln *must* have a black beard, any believable 1950s Marilyn Monroe *must* have wavy platinum-blonde hair.

Volumes have been written about the intricacies of stage makeup, and there are now numerous instructional videos available that explain shading, contours, color schemes, facial maps, light zones, reshaping, and more. Makeup needs for most children's plays can be met by using a combination of the basics: **greasepaint** or **pancake makeup** for the foundation supplemented by powder, rouge, lipstick, mascara, eyebrow, or shadow liner. Cold cream is the best remover for makeup, and **spirit gum** works well for securing beards and mustaches and big ears (don't forget the spirit gum remover!). Nose putty, liquid latex, and tooth wax can create some interesting effects. Bald caps, scarring liquid, hair coloring sprays, stage blood, even body powder are available from commercial sources, quite possibly in your own area.

Most likely, your makeup artist will be an adult volunteer with enough experience and patience to work some minimal magic on your actors' otherwise normal young faces. As with costuming, it's very useful to draw up a **makeup chart** for each character that tells what sort of makeup, wiggery, or hair styling they'll need.

Lights

The fundamental purpose of theatre lighting is to show the actors to the audience, particularly the actors' faces and expressions. Lighting can also be used to convey mood, time of day, or geographic locale. Spotlighting an actor highlights that actor in a specific moment in time, telling the audience that this is a very special person performing a very special act — even if it's simply standing silently in the middle of the stage.

Some of the scripts you work with will have detailed lighting instructions you can follow; many scripts won't. And if you write your own original play, you'll have to come up with your own original lighting plan as well.

Naturally, it makes a difference if you're doing the play inside or outside. If outside at noon, clearly, you won't have to worry much about artificial lighting. However, if showtime is at dusk or after dark, a lighting system of some kind becomes necessary just so the actors can find their way around the stage.

If you're doing the play inside, are there windows? If you require complete darkness at some point, these light sources will need to be covered, especially during daylight. Then again, the window light may not matter or may even be a good mood-setter in terms of the play's story.

The director's initial task is to decide what lighting is crucial to the play's performance. Go through the script and mark where lighting cues exist. Many plays can be performed without any special lighting effects or light changes other than turning the room lights on and off between scenes. With most children's plays, the action, dialogue, and story line are the most important elements of the event, and lack of sophisticated lighting won't seriously diminish anyone's enjoyment.

But...great and imaginative lighting *can* wonderfully enhance your play as well as offer valuable technical training to eager young crew members. Weigh your budget, timetable, and volunteer expertise options to decide how big a role lighting will play in the production.

If you're performing in an auditorium of some kind, a house lighting system is usually available — maybe just a set of recessed ceiling lights above the stage or maybe a spotlight or two or a small set of border striplights or footlights. Work with it and see if it satisfies your play's lighting needs. Do lights need to dim down and fade up during a scene? Do you need to spotlight certain characters at certain times that keep certain parts of the stage in darkness while others are in varying degrees of light? Do you need special effects that simulate lightning, explosions, aurora borealis, the Last Judgment?

If so, then you need to visit a stage equipment rental store or peruse a stage equipment catalogue...and seek aid from the lighting designer at your local high school or college or professional theatre.

It's important to decide *where* you want the light to come from. You can light the stage from directly above and have the light shine onto the stage below (Fig. 32).

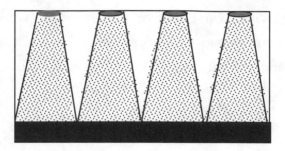

FIG.32. LIGHTING FROM DIRECTLY ABOVE STAGE (FRONT VIEW)

You can light it from the front with lights hanging from a batten attached to the ceiling (Fig. 33).

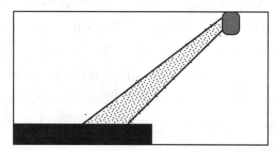

FIG.33. LIGHTING FROM FRONT AND ABOVE (SIDE VIEW)

You can light it from the side with either lights attached to a ceiling bar or lights attached to a **"tree"** that stands on the floor (Fig. 34).

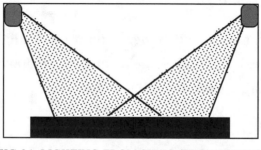

FIG.34. LIGHTING FROM SIDES (FRONT VIEW)

You can light it from the back of the room with a big **follow spotlight** casting a beam that can be narrowed and widened by hand (Fig. 35).

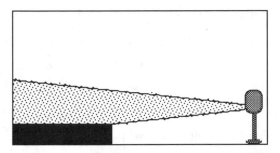

FIG.35. LIGHTING FROM BACK WITH FOLLOW SPOTLIGHT (SIDE VIEW)

Or you can use a combination and have **fill lighting** from behind or sides or floor to supplement your main lights (Fig. 36).

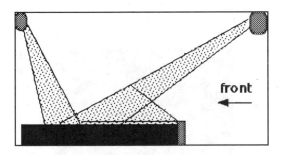

FIG.36. LIGHTING FROM BEHIND, BELOW, AND ABOVE FRONT
(SIDE VIEW)

Once you've decided what parts of the stage you want lit and where the light should come from, you have several options as far as equipment, all depending on your budget, crew capacity, and the structural ability of the room. Make sure the room you're performing in can handle the additional electrical load lights draw.

You can get **floodlights** (scoop or olivette), **spotlights** (focus, fresnel, ellipsoidal, plano-convex or follow), **beamlights**, **halogen lights**, **striplights** (footlights, border lights, backing lights, or horizon lights) and **reflector lights**. Each type has its own characteristics that make it well-suited for some lighting situations and not so well-suited for others. For further variety, you can cover a light lens with a thin-sheeted colored filter called a **gel** (short for gelatin, the material from which they're made) or a circular piece of colored glass called a **roundel** or make your own **gobos** — aluminum sheets with cut-out patterns that cast a simple pattern on the reflected beam: a window, a crucifix, a word, a boat, and so on.

Modern stage lighting setups are regulated by **switchboards** that generally include dimmer controls as well as switches for turning lights on and off. You can even **pre-set** your light cues — record them into the switchboard's electronic memory and punch them up when needed.

The director will want to notate the light cues in the script. Some light operators prefer to work from a notated script, while others desire a separate **light cue chart** (Fig. 37).

LIGHT CUE CHART

PLAY TITLE: **How the People Got Fire**

Cue #	Page #	Light Effect
1	1	lights fade up right on Narrator
2	1	lights quickly up left on Mother and Child
3	2	spotlight on Toyeskom entering from left; follow to corncobs
4	2	crossfade: lights dim left on People, lights up right on Thunder & Lightning
5	3	effect: lightning flashes as Thunder & Lightning dance (strobe)
6		
7		
8		

FIG.37. LIGHT CUE CHART

Sound

The main "sound" of a play is the actor's voices speaking dialogue. But a play can also have other sounds: songs, instrumental music, or various **sound effects** that make the play's setting more realistic, advance the plot, or add another dimension to the character's personality.

Let's look at sound effects first. A sound effect is an off-stage sound (usually) that makes the audience think they hear something that occurs in the naturalistic world of the play — a gunshot, a hurricane, a bugle, a telephone, a cow, a siren, a Shriners' convention, a waterfall. Some sound effects are meant to be heard "in the distance"; others are meant to be heard as if they were part of the live action onstage.

As with lighting, some of the scripts you work with will have instructions for sound cues; many scripts won't. The director should go through the script and mark where sound cues exist, then begin figuring out how to create them. You have a lot of latitude here.

Some plays have actors make sound effects with their voices or by striking things on or offstage. This can be intentionally humorous when actors knock on the nearest wood when entering a room, use their vocal apparatus to blare trumpet fanfares, make engine noises and mimic the wind, or clap their hands sharply when a pistol rings out.

Or you can have a sound crew offstage making sounds with objects that simulate the real action, as was done to near perfection in the days of radio dramas. These homemade sound effects are fun to dream up and perform. Try making a "rain box" (wooden box filled with dried peas or rice), a "thunder sheet" (a large, thin metal sheet shaken by hand or tapped with a percussion mallet) or "sea sieve" (very small pieces of lead shot swirled about in a sieve or pan).

Need a quick car crash? Fill a bucket with broken glass or dish fragments and pour it quickly into another bucket. How about galloping horses? Knock two coconut shells or wood blocks against the floor...for a horse trotting on wet ground or grass, cover the floor with a towel or piece of carpet. Swooping helicopter? Get an electric table fan and an electric shaver; turn the shaver on and hold it in front of the fast-moving fan blades so its steady drone is "chopped up" to resemble the whirling arms of the copter. Use your imagination!

If you want truly realistic sound effects, you can record the actual sounds on tapes or mini-discs and play them at the appropriate moment of the action. Many sound effect records and compact discs exist for this purpose. Compiling these and playing them during the show using a cassette, CD, or mini-disc player would be the job of your sound director. Notating the sound cues in the script is vital; compiling a **sound cue chart** (Fig. 38) is also helpful.

<u>**SOUND CUE CHART**</u>

PLAY TITLE: **How the People Got Fire**

<u>Cue #</u>	<u>Page #</u>	<u>Duration</u>	<u>Sound Effect</u>
1	1	20 sec.	Song of the Embers—live flute OS
2	2	8 sec.	drumming OS when Toyeskom enters
3	2	5 sec.	thunder sheet OS when Thunder & Lightning enter
4	3	5 sec.	tape cue #1: eagle screech when Woswosim enters
5	3	5 sec.	tape cue #2: coyote howl when Coyote enters
6	5	6-8 sec.	Song of the Embers, first 2 bars—live flute OS
7			

FIG.38. SOUND CUE CHART

Depending on how large your room is, you might have to have your live offstage sound effects performed into a microphone so they can be heard by the audience. This brings us to the subject of sound amplification systems.

You may be performing in a room that has a built-in sound system, which could range from a single microphone attached to a floor stand that runs through a two-channel stereo amplifier and comes out of a pair of tinny overhead speakers...to a state-of-the-art lavaliere or head mike setup mixed and equalized through a multi-channel soundboard that distributes the sound throughout the room via a ring of acoustically balanced, carefully placed speakers. We can dream...

Most kids' plays won't have access to a very extensive sound system. If you have one microphone, it might come in handy for the Narrator, who is likely to be stationary through most of the play. There's no point in passing the mike around or hanging it from the ceiling to pick up a wide area of sound or catch an actor as they wander by...doesn't work. You simply have to encourage the actors to face toward the audience, speak loudly and pro-*JECT*. And ask your audience to sit as close as possible. Remember, Shakespeare didn't have a sound system, either.

Some plays have songs or instrumental music. If you're not using a sound system, you may want to position your singers and musicians onstage, even if they're not in the direct action of the play, so they can be better heard by the audience and actors. The objective here is to balance the volume of a vocal chorus and musical ensemble with the spoken dialogue, making sure the singing and music support but do not overwhelm the actors' words.

A Final Thought on Tech Stuff

Fancy whizbangs and high-res geegaws aren't going to make your play a success. It's the power of the acting that will grab the audience most forcefully and leave them with the strongest impression of what your play has said. Use enough technology to help the actors feel in the spirit of the play and to be seen and heard by the audience; but, frankly, the less tech stuff you *have* to use, the better off you are.

Booklist for Technical Advice

Newspaper Theatre by Alice Morin. Belmont, Calif.: Fearon Teacher Aids, 1989 (500 Harbor Boulevard, Belmont, CA, 94002).

Creative Costumes for Children without Sewing by Mark Walker. Boca Raton, Fla.: Cool Hand Communications, 1993 (1098 N.W. Boca Raton Blvd., #1, Boca Raton, FL, 33432).

Self-Supporting Scenery by James Hull Miller. Colorado Springs, Colo.: Meriwether Publishing, 1987 (P.O. Box 7710, Colorado Springs, CO, 80933).

Creative Theatrical Makeup by Donna J. Arnink. Englewood Cliffs, N.J.: Prentice-Hall, 1984.

Stage Properties and How to Make Them by Warren Kenton. London, England: Pitman Publishing, 1978.

Create Your Own Stage Props by Jacquie Govier. Englewood Cliffs, N.J.: Prentice-Hall, 1984.

Part Six
REHEARSING THE SHOW

You've erected your stage, chosen your tech crew, pulled together the necessary equipment — now it's time to begin rehearsing the play.

The rehearsal process proceeds through four distinct phases:

1. reading and blocking — showing actors what to say and where to move

2. interpreting character — showing actors how to speak and move

3. technical rehearsal — making sure the machinery and tech stuff works

4. dress rehearsal — making sure everything and everyone works

Depending upon your play's complexity and your company's availability, you may want to spend two rehearsals on reading and blocking, three on interpreting character, two on technical, and just one dress rehearsal. Or your technical and dress rehearsals may be combined into one last-minute pulling-it-all-together session. It's up to you as director to assess what your play needs at any given point in the rehearsal schedule.

If your actors are also helping out with making costumes and scenery, you may want to set separate rehearsals to work on these areas.

First Rehearsal: Reading and Blocking

The director should gather the actors and have them sit comfortably in a circle to read through the play again together. Everyone has a script, of course (stapled scripts will be easier to work with when moving around onstage). Allow exaggerations during the reading. Kids love bug eyes, horse laughs, silly expressions. You'll use these in the Second Rehearsal.

Talk about relationships between characters: Does Character A like Character B? What does Character C want from Character D? Read the script through again and have everyone act out motions. Have the actors think about what each scene looks like; have them imagine what objects are in the scene and how they might be constructed.

Read through the script at least twice. Once the actors are straight on pronunciation, appear to be familiarizing themselves with the rhythm and flow of the dialogue, and have some ideas about how their characters sound, move and think, you can move on to **blocking**.

Blocking is the process of showing actors where and how they move during the play. Your task as director will be made easier if you have a clear idea of what happens to whom when. Basically, you become a traffic cop, but your objectivity in seeing how the play unfolds is crucial. You are, during rehearsal, the stand-in for the audience.

Your first task as director, then, is to understand yourself where the actors stand, how they enter and exit, when they cross from one part of the stage to another and by what path. Go through the script and make diagrams at various points that show exactly where the actors are. You'll quickly form a mental map of these movements, but it never hurts to have some written reference point.

Blocking will depend upon space. Try to rehearse where you'll be performing. If this is not possible, measure the performing space and try to approximate it as closely as possible in terms of width and length. Mark out the perimeter of the acting area with tape or chalk or simply by boundary landmarks such as chairs or lamps. This is a good time to remind the actors of the basic stage areas — upstage, downstage, right, left, and so on — and then show them where these areas are in your particular acting area. You can draw or tape the stage areas on the floor if you like.

For the first blocking **walk-through**, have the actors carry their scripts with them so they can mark down positions. Some handy abbreviations commonly used to denote stage movement include:

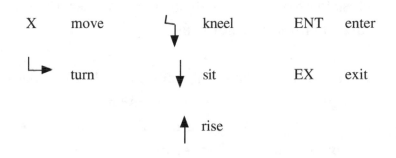

X	move		kneel	ENT	enter
	turn		sit	EX	exit
			rise		

Your bright, eager children will no doubt be able to memorize their blocking very quickly, but it doesn't hurt to help them increase their theatrical self-awareness by encouraging them to be responsible for their own onstage whereabouts and notate their scripts.

Some additional shorthand terms you'll find useful in communicating with your actors:

- move up — move upstage, away from the audience

- move down — move downstage, toward the audience

- move forward — move forward in the direction you're facing

- move backward — move backward from the direction you're facing

- open up — turn your body toward the audience

- close in — turn your body away from the audience, usually toward center stage

Any director of kids' plays will want to study the blocking and staging methods used by **Readers Theatre**. Readers Theatre is a style of presenting literature — most often poems, short stories, novel excerpts, radio plays — as a staged play. Readers Theatre doesn't use much scenery, costuming, makeup, or sound and light effects; rather, it communicates through characterization: The gestures, expressions, vocal interpretations and movements of the actors are very important and are aided by clever blocking designs and interweavings created by the director. Readers Theatre is a good example of how a small company can effectively put a play across with very little technical resources.

After you've done a first blocking, try running the play from beginning to end with kids incorporating the blocking as they read from the script. Take small bits at a time and go over difficult spots as often as you need. Actors learning their lines usually paraphrase at first; prompt them with the correct lines, gently but insistently. If an actor is having a really difficult time saying the right lines, take them aside individually later on and work through the problem.

Above all, remind kids to listen to each other. Acting is to a large degree *re*-acting, and each actor must be fully engaged in what everyone else is doing onstage at every moment.

Now, take a break and gather the whole company around: It's time for the director to give **director's notes**. These are observations the director has made on the execution of acting and technical cues. For the most part, they are repetitions of things the director has already said and will need to affirm repeatedly ("Jenna, please make sure to turn your head to the left when addressing the Count"), or they may be changes in script or blocking ("let's have the Archers kneel instead of stand this time") or even the airing of questions about a particular issue or point in the play ("if the Giraffe stands at mid left and the Monkey at mid right and they're supposed to talk to each other, would it be better if they stood closer?").

In giving your notes, Mr./Ms. Director, you must be patient and gentle in delivery but completely concise and detailed in your explanations of what you want to happen onstage. Help the actors see what you see, feel what you feel. Remember, you are functioning as a future audience.

Try another **run** all the way through if you have time. Before you send everyone home, remind your actors to memorize their lines — completely — for next rehearsal. A helpful technique is for actors to record their lines on tape, play them back and listen to themselves or speak along. Encourage the children to rehearse on their own, with siblings, friends, parents. Pair up your actors, with one child reciting from memory while another prompts and corrects, then switching places.

SCRIPT	MOVES	CUES	NOTES
(LIGHTS UP RIGHT on BACCHUS standing at down right, toying with a bunch of grapes.)		flute music OS ends when Bacc. speaks	
BACCHUS: *(to audience)* Hello. How do you do? I am Bacchus, god of revelry and wine. You do not recognize me? For shame! For we have met together many a time!			Bacc. offers grapes to audience
With my fermented fruit, I bring joy to your nights Though your head may ache sore in the morning. Too many sips, and over you tip— Good judgment flees without warning!			
Men round the world pay homage to me, Craving the juice from the vine; Believing themselves mighty and bold, While they stumble, feeble and blind.	Bacc. X DC		Bacc. holds up grapes
Let me tell you the story of a King Who lived in Phrygia long centuries ago. Midas was his name, and oft-sad he was For of money he always ran low. *(exits right)*	Bacc. ⌐▶ DR		
(LIGHTS UP CENTER AND LEFT; KING MIDAS sits on large chair at mid center, his BURSAR standing at his right holding a quill pen and an open accounting book.)			KM stressed; Bur. timid
KING MIDAS: No, it cannot be! It cannot be at all! The treasury is nearly empty again, And more creditors come to call?			
BURSAR: My King, you are a glorious king Who has won many a war and battle. But the way this kingdom runs through gold It's like feeding turnips to cattle!			

FIG.39. PROMPT SCRIPT

IMPORTANT! Don't forget that the director should keep a **prompt script** — a three-ring-binder copy of the script that is, in effect, the master version containing all dialogue, blocking, light, sound, and tech cues along with any other notes the director makes during rehearsals (Fig. 39). Typically, the stage manager or assistant stage manager maintains the prompt script, but it's a wise idea for a director to have instant access to it as well.

Second Rehearsal: Interpreting Character

After starting off with some vocal and movement warmup exercises, the director can begin working with interpretation of character — facial expressions, vocal projection, articulation, correct body movements. These elements may have already surfaced during the first rehearsal read-through when you encouraged actors to "ham it up" and explore their characters' physicality and emotion.

In terms of rehearsal format, do as many runs as time allows. Have as many props ready for use as you can muster; ditto for any song, dance, and music segments that need to be integrated into the action. Hopefully, all lines are completely memorized and the actors can concentrate less on prompting and more on delving into their character.

For most kids, getting into a character and staying there isn't an automatic deal — not in front of grown-ups, anyway. As director, the main challenge will be getting your young actors to forget any residual shyness and consistently deliver their lines with the right emphasis and inflection, i.e., to act "naturally" and feel "in the moment" at a moment's notice.

Ask the child to think about what the words mean before speaking them. "Say it like you mean it!" is a good rule to cite. Have the child pretend he *is* the character and encourage him to "get in character": talking, walking, eating, drinking, laughing, sneezing as if he were that person or animal. Try having actors stay in character throughout the rehearsal; it can be enlightening as well as humorous.

If your play deals with a certain culture or historical period, it would be a good idea to bring in books, recordings, and even films with examples of how those characters speak, dress, and move.

A suggestion for helping kids focus on being "in the moment": if your actors are getting distracted, have them picture that they are performing in a space bounded by four walls, four blank walls that separate them from everything else in the room.

On the other hand, you may have a play that dispenses with the fourth wall and directs that your actors speak *directly* to the audience, as if the audience and their reaction were a scripted part of the play. Which, in some instances, they are.

This no-fourth-wall style of presentation can prove challenging to novice actors — and directors. But, if you've had your actors learn a monologue or two during their pre-rehearsal training, they should at least possess the mental concept of a missing fourth wall.

Projection problems? Have the actors pretend they're saying their lines to the only person in the room — a very old person who is very hard of hearing sitting wayyyyyyyyyyyyyyy at the veryveryvery back...talk to that person so they can hear you.

But projection doesn't mean mindless shrieking or bellowing. While volume is important, so is the articulation and enunciation of the words the actor is speaking. Refer back to the inflection exercise in Part Three, if necessary. And remind actors to sustain their lines to the end of their delivery, especially while exiting, to avoid "swallowing their lines."

The main point to emphasize to actors through rehearsal and during director's notes is this: A good actor is one the audience believes to be *not* acting. A newsgirl entering the scene shouldn't drag across stage mumbling to the floor as if she were looking for a lost button: "Extra! Extra! Suitor Found for Boss' Daughter! Read all about it!" She should stride across stage, head raised, eyes wide, arms outstretched as if calling out the headlines were the most important thing happening in the whole world at that very moment.

Which, in the world of her character, it *is*.

An important and often overlooked element of characterization is **business** — the physical activities, aside from movement, that an actor performs to emphasize the realism of the character.

Necessary business comes naturally from the action of the play; **imposed business** is what an actor does to enhance the nature of the character or add an element of interpretation to the story line. The following excerpt has both kinds of business:

JESSE JAMES: Reckon I'll help Mrs. James with the housework. *(pulls handkerchief from back pocket and mimes dusting a picture, turning his back to the Fords)* Don't tell her I'm making her pictures crooked.

(Charlie and Robert Ford look at each other, Charlie motioning Robert to pull his pistol; Robert Ford pulls his pistol, aims at Jesse's head, and shoots. SOUND: gun shot. Jesse falls to floor as Mrs. Jesse James turns and kneels at Jesse's side.)

ROBERT FORD: It was an accident!

MRS. JESSE JAMES: An accident on purpose! You traitor! Robert Ford, traitor! May you and your brother never know a moment of peace! *(lets dish she's holding fall to the floor)*

When Robert Ford pulls the pistol and shoots Jesse James, his handling, aiming, and shooting of the gun is necessary business. When Jesse James pulls out his handkerchief and dusts the picture he's in the process of straightening, that's imposed business, as is Mrs. Jesse James dropping the dish to emphasize her cursing of the Fords.

Business should never distract the actor or audience from the story line. If you have a line of royal guards standing next to the throne, they should probably just stand at attention rather than polish their swords or adjust their helmet straps.

Yet, having a fairy godmother enter, pause, and wave her magic wand for a few seconds before proceeding into her dialogue is a quick way of communicating something about her character to the audience, as well as foreshadowing the fact that the wand might be of some major importance later on.

Your goal by the end of Rehearsal #2 is to have the actors able to perform the play without stopping. The director must be very alert at this stage to make certain all actors fully understand their roles and their blocking. Before calling it quits for this rehearsal, ask *several times* if anyone has *any* questions.

Because the company's attention will now turn to tech stuff...

Third Rehearsal: Integrating Tech Stuff

A **technical rehearsal** is when backstage meets onstage — lighting, sound, and scenery movement are integrated into the total production and any technical problems in these areas are solved.

The first tech run-through is often done without the actors and is typically overseen by the stage manager or technical director, though the director will always want to keep close tabs on what's happening. Lights are mounted and focused, the stage and scenery moved into place, sound players or sound effect makers readied.

The crew members proceed through the cue and scene changes, pausing when necessary to work out any problems. This is also a good time to **spike** the floor — mark the position of set pieces with small bits of masking tape.

The second tech run-through has the actors onstage performing the play, again stopping the action as needed to make sure all technical elements are in synch.

Finally there's the **costume parade**, where actors walk in costume under the stage lights to make sure everything that needs to be seen is seen and everything that shouldn't be seen isn't. This is a good chance for the costumer and director to make any changes in costume before the final dress rehearsal.

Fourth Rehearsal: Places, Everyone!

The **dress rehearsal** is an actual performance of the play with all elements in place — except the audience. Usually held the night before the play's public opening, a dress rehearsal has actors dressed in full costume and makeup and all technical cues ready to roll. Don't forget to rehearse the **curtain call** at the end of the play!

Now is a good time to acquaint the company with the system of **calls** employed in the theatre. There is the **crew call**, which is the time crew members are supposed to arrive at the theatre to begin preparing for the play; a **cast call** is when actors are supposed to be on hand. Usually, you want everyone on hand an hour before the play is set to begin; possibly your tech people may need to be there a bit earlier. Make sure these call times are established at the end of the dress rehearsal.

On the night of the show after the cast and crew have arrived, the stage manager gives a series of **time calls** that are warnings announcing how much time is left before the curtain rises. At these intervals the stage manager goes around the theatre to each member of the crew and cast and calls out the time: "30 minutes. 30 minutes, please." Other calls are given at 15 minutes, 5 minutes, and finally — a minute or so before the play starts — "Places! Places, everyone!"

Which means all actors and crew members are in place and ready to begin the play.

Break a leg!

Following the show, the director will assemble the company and give director's notes, noting any areas for improvement or change and giving LOTS of encouragement and affirmation to everybody's contribution.

And, after the last performance of your play, the stage manager will supervise the cast and crew as they **strike** (remove) all the scenery, props, costumes, and equipment. The stage is dismantled, set pieces stored, borrowed items returned, sponsors thanked, memories neatly folded and tucked away for some future glimpse back into the past...

Part Seven
DON'T FORGET THE AUDIENCE

Your play is ready to roll, and your company is eager to perform. What's next?

You'll likely want to start small, maybe performing just for your immediate family and a few friends and neighbors. The children will want to do it again, and then you could invite a few more friends and neighbors and perform at a major social function like a neighborhood barbecue or yard sale. Other parents might become interested, and then you're talking about the Big Time: Cub Scouts and Brownies or even a church group or senior citizen center and then down the Yellow Brick Road to local fairs, libraries — The Mall!

You'd be amazed at how enthusiastically people welcome free entertainment.

Back to current reality. Your first show is tonight, and you've got everything lined up: chair and room setup, location of fire exits, a ticket seller and ushers, programs, refreshments, and provisions for post-show cleanup.

But before this, you've already taken care of the first order of business, haven't you...publicizing the play and getting an audience?

The simplest way is to create a **mailing flyer**, a one-page announcement that supplies information about the performance's What, When, Where, Who, and How Much.

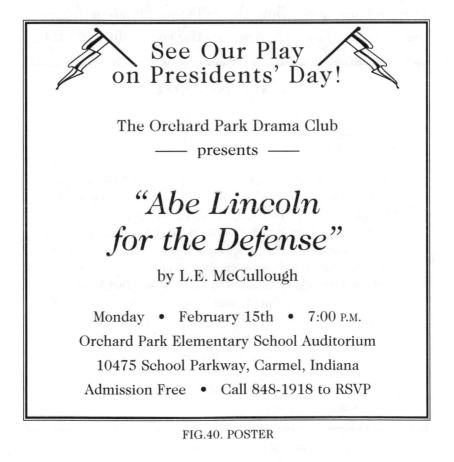

See Our Play
on Presidents' Day!

The Orchard Park Drama Club
—— presents ——

"Abe Lincoln for the Defense"

by L.E. McCullough

Monday • February 15th • 7:00 P.M.
Orchard Park Elementary School Auditorium
10475 School Parkway, Carmel, Indiana
Admission Free • Call 848-1918 to RSVP

FIG.40. POSTER

You can have a child or two contribute a drawing and some lettering if you like, but no matter how "artistic" you make the flyer, be sure the time, date, location (directions if necessary), and information phone number for tickets or reservations are legibly displayed. Also an admission charge, if applicable, as well as the name of your company or sponsoring organization.

Depending upon how large an audience you want, you can stuff these in neighbor doors, mail them as invitations to friends, give them to people at work, or have kids pass them out at school. (Don't actually put them *in* mailboxes; the U.S. Postal Service reserves the sole right to do this!)

** News Release**

To: Arts/Life Style Editor
From: Jane Whelchel, (317) 848-1353
Date: 1/15/99

See history come alive with the Orchard Park Drama Club's Presidents 'Day performance of *Abe Lincoln for the Defense!*, a play by popular children's author L.E. McCullough, Monday, Feb. 15 at 7 p.m. in the Orchard Park Elementary School auditorium, 10475 School Parkway in Carmel, Indiana. Admission is free; call 848-1918 to reserve seats.

Abe Lincoln for the Defense! is based on a true event — young attorney Abraham Lincoln's brilliant courtroom defense of Duff Armstrong, a family friend accused of murder and faced with seemingly irrefutable evidence of guilt.

The Orchard Park Drama Club is made up of 5th grade students supervised by Orchard Park Elementary teachers Linda Warder and Diana Gillespie. The students use plays to enhance their learning of subjects in history, social studies, and environmental science.

Photos available upon request.

FIG.41. PRESS RELEASE FOR NEWSPAPERS

If you are doing a serious fundraiser and want lots of folks attending, you'll need to whip up a **news release** that you'll send to your local print and broadcast media (Fig. 41). Keep the news release short — one page at most, unless you've got an astronaut or movie star dropping by, which would clearly be highly newsworthy and merit a second page.

For newspapers, you'll send the release to Arts Editor or Calendar Editor or Features Editor. The news release you send to radio or television stations has traditionally been called a **public service announcement** or **PSA** (Fig. 42). These are read in "community calendar" segments between programs and therefore can't be more than 30 seconds in length or they won't get read on the air.

** PSA — 20 Seconds **

To: PSA–Community Calender
From: Jane Whelchel, (317) 848-1353
Date: 1/15/99

SEE HISTORY COME ALIVE WITH THE **ORCHARD PARK DRAMA CLUB'S** PERFORMANCE OF "***ABE LINCOLN FOR THE DEFENSE!***," A SPECIAL PRESIDENTS' DAY PLAY RUNNING MONDAY, FEB. 15 AT 7 P.M. IN THE ORCHARD PARK ELEMENTARY SCHOOL AUDITORIUM, 10475 SCHOOL PARKWAY IN CARMEL. ADMISSION IS FREE; CALL 848-1918 TO RESERVE SEATS.

FIG.42. PSA FOR RADIO AND TELEVISION STATIONS

All right, you've sent out your publicity, and your audience is on its way. A good two hours before showtime, the house crew under the guidance of the house manager have set to work preparing the room:

- The stage has been situated, along with any lights, sound, electrical, or special effect equipment to be used .

- The tech table has been set up to the side or in the back where light and sound operators will sit and work their wizardry.

- The restrooms have been cleaned and all floors and seats have been tidied up.

- The audience seating has been arranged, including an unobstructed path to at least one exit clearly marked by a large EXIT sign.

- A highly visible NO SMOKING, HUMANS PRESENT sign is on display.

- Refreshments are ready at the concession table.

- Ushers are armed with programs and smiles.

- The ticket seller is waiting outside the door with a roll of tickets and a box full of small bills.

- The master of ceremonies is prepared to step up onstage and extend an official welcome to the audience before the play begins.

- The cleanup crew knows exactly who they are, what to do and where to put it after the show.

Everything in place? Congratulations! You are ready to open the house!

Part Eight
THREE PLAYS —
FROM TOP TO BOTTOM

These three plays are presented in detail so you can get a sense of how a play unfolds. The format is simple: dialogue and stage directions are on the left side of the page...the right side of the page offers suggested director's notes on blocking and interpretation, with diagrams supplementing the description.

The first play, *Little Orphant Annie*, is a simple word-and-motion play perfect for Grades K–1. It requires no scenery other than a stool, and costuming is also minimal. Actors can use basic miming gestures with a bit of improvisation as they interpret the words of the poem.

The second play, *How the People Got Fire*, works well for Grades 2–4. It adds some scenery, props, and simple masks and body costumes along with lighting and sound effects.

The third play, *The Story of Silent Night*, is a short three-scene piece for Grades 5–7. It features period costume, choral song, and the opportunity for a good deal of emotive, realistic acting.

Little Orphant Annie
adapted by L.E. McCullough

This play is an adaptation of a popular poem by James Whitcomb Riley (1849–1916), who was born in Greenfield, Indiana, and lived much of his adult life in Indianapolis. Before he achieved fame as a poet and lecturer, Riley worked as a shoe store clerk, Bible salesman, house painter, medicine show entertainer, and newspaper writer.

Little Orphant Annie was a based on a real orphan girl who had stayed at the Riley farm when Riley was a boy. It was first published in 1885 as *The Elf Child* in the *Indianapolis Journal* newspaper and quickly became a highlight of Riley's public poetry readings.

Riley was a close observer of ordinary people and their habits, especially the ways in which they talked. The characters here speak in a distinctive "Hoosier" dialect that uses grammar and pronounciation common to many Midwestern country people during the late 1800s. For today's children, the dialect of *Little Orphant Annie* provides a very good exercise in spelling and enunciation. Have the actors speak slowly and with great emphasis on each syllable; this will impart clarity to the words (which enhances comprehension) and a singsong rhythm to the phrasing (which adds dramatic effect).

Most likely the real Little Orphant Annie didn't know how to read and write — but she sure knew how to tell a scary story!

CAST: Little Orphant Annie
      Naughty Boy
      Naughty Girl
      Four Children
      Mammy
      Daddy
      Two Big Black Things

SET: a stool at mid center

PROPS: a pair of pants

COSTUMES: simple everyday clothing for Mammy, Daddy, Naughty Boy, Naughty Girl, and Four Children. Little Orphant Annie can wear a bonnet or old-fashioned feathered hat with an apron. Big Black Things dress in black and wear black hoods.

*LIGHTS UP FULL on stool at mid center. **Four Children** stand around the stool in a trapezoidal perimeter and address audience. (FIG. 1, page 116)*

CHILD 1
"Little Orphant Annie" is the play we bring,

CHILD 2
From a poem by James Whitcomb Riley;

CHILD 3
We hope it finds you in good cheer,

CHILD 4
And leaves you warm and smiley!

CHILD 1
Little Orphant Annie's
Come to our house to stay,
An' wash the cups an' saucers up,
An' brush the crumbs away,
An' shoo the chickens off the porch,
An' dust the hearth, an' sweep,
An' make the fire, an' bake the bread,
An' earn her board an' keep.

(FIG. 2) **Little Orphant Annie** enters from right; she mimes washing, brushing, shooing, sweeping her way to down center, then sits on stool.

CHILD 2
An' all us other children,
When the supper things is done,
We set around the kitchen fire
An' has the mostest fun
A-list'nin' to the witch-tales
That Annie tells about—

Children 1-4 gather closer around **Annie**, who slaps her knee and puts an index finger to her cheek as if thinking of a new story.

LITTLE ORPHANT ANNIE

An' the Gobble-uns that gits you
Ef you
Don't
Watch
Out!

CHILD 3

Wunst they wuz a little boy
Wouldn't say his prayers,
An' when he went to bed at night,
Away up stairs,
His Mammy heerd him holler,
An' his Daddy heerd him bawl,
An' when they turn't the kivvers
  down,
He wuzn't there at all!

CHILD 4

An' they seeked him in the
  rafter-room,
An' cubby hole, an' press,
An' seeked him up the chimbly-flue,
An' ever'wheres, I guess;
But all they ever found wuz
Just his pants an' roundabout;

LITTLE ORPHANT ANNIE

An' the Gobble-uns'll git you
Ef you
Don't
Watch
Out!

CHILD 1

An' one time a little girl
Woud always laugh an' grin,
An' make fun of ever'one,
An' all her blood an' kin;

Annie frowns and shakes a finger at
Children, who shrink slightly away
from her.

(FIG. 3) **Naughty Boy** enters from
right, stomping and angry, and moves
across to down left; he is followed
onstage by exasperated **Mammy** and
Daddy who stand at down right, their
hands folded in prayer; **Naughty Boy**
mockingly waves them away and
turns away to stage left; he suddenly
shouts in terror and leaps offstage left
as if being swept off his feet.

(FIG. 4) **Mammy** and **Daddy** startle
at the shout and peer about the stage
for **Naughty Boy**; **Mammy** crosses
toward left, going up center and
behind stool searching; **Daddy**
crosses toward left, going down center in front of stool searching;
Mammy and **Daddy** bump into each
other at down left, are startled, and
then look down at floor; **Daddy** picks
up a pair of pants and holds them
forlornly as **Mammy** weeps; **Mammy**
and **Daddy** exit left as **Annie**
solemnly lectures **Children**.

(FIG. 5) **Naughty Girl** enters from
right, skipping and giggling, and
moves across to down left passing
the Children, making faces at them,
sticking out her tongue, wiggling her
fingers, and laughing meanly.

An' wunst, when they wuz company,
An' ole folks wuz there,
She mocked 'em an' shocked 'em,
An' said she didn't care!

CHILD 2
An' just as she kicked her heels,
An' turn't to run an' hide,
They wuz two great big Black Things
A-standin' by her side,
An' they snatched her through the
     ceilin'
Fore she knowed what she's about!

(FIG. 6) **Naughty Girl** mockingly
curtsies and turns away to stage left;
she suddenly shrieks in terror and is
whisked offstage left by **Two Big
Black Things**.

LITTLE ORPHANT ANNIE
An' the Gobble-uns'll git you
Ef you
Don't
Watch
Out!

Annie stands and solemnly lectures
Children.

CHILD 3
An' Little Orphant Annie says,
When the blaze is blue,

Child 3 takes a step forward.

CHILD 4
An' the lamp-wick sputters,
An' the wind goes *woo-oo!*

Child 4 takes a step forward.

CHILDREN 1-4
Woo-oo!

Children 1-4 crouch and slowly rise
as they *Woo-oo!*

CHILD 3
An' you hear the crickets quit,
An' the moon is gray,

Child 3 takes a step forward.

CHILD 4
An' the lightnin' bugs in dew
Is all squenched away,

Child 4 takes a step forward.

LITTLE ORPHANT ANNIE
You better mind yer parents
An' yer teachers fond an' dear,
An' cherish them that loves you,
An' dry the orphant's tear,
An' help the pore an' needy ones
That clusters all about,
Er the Gobble-uns'll git you

CHILD 1
Ef—

CHILD 2
You—

CHILD 3
Don't—

CHILD 4
Watch—

ENTIRE CAST
Out!

LIGHTS OUT.

THE END.

(FIG. 7) **Annie** and **Children 1-4** are at down center in even line across stage facing audience; **Annie** turns to right and addresses **Children 1 and 3**.

Annie turns to left and addresses **Children 2 and 4**.

Child 1 speaks then turns back to audience.

Child 2 speaks then turns back to audience.

Child 3 speaks then turns back to audience.

Child 4 speaks then turns back to audience.

Children 1-4 turn and shout at audience as **Annie** places hat over her face and **Entire Cast** freezes in place.

Stage Plan — *Little Orphant Annie*

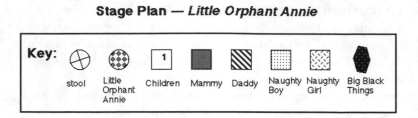

Key: stool | Little Orphant Annie | Children | Mammy | Daddy | Naughty Boy | Naughty Girl | Big Black Things

FIG.1: Positions at Opening Setting.

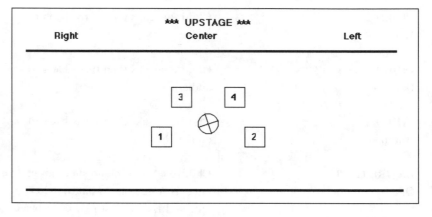

FIG.2: Little Orphant Annie enters from right and sits on stool.

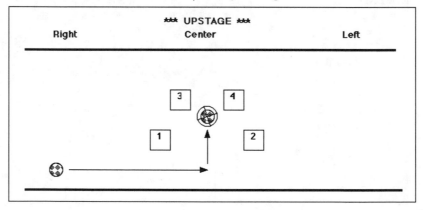

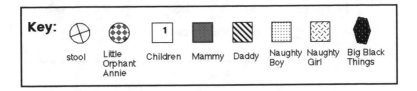

Key: stool / Little Orphant Annie / Children / Mammy / Daddy / Naughty Boy / Naughty Girl / Big Black Things

FIG.3: *Naughty Boy enters from right and crosses to down left, followed by Mammy and Daddy who pause at down right as Naughty Boy waves mockingly; after waving, Naughty Boy is whisked offstage left.*

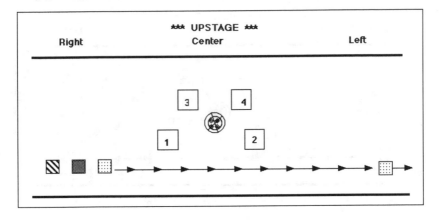

FIG.4: *Mammy and Daddy cross stage searching for Naughty Boy, end up at down left and find pants before exiting left.*

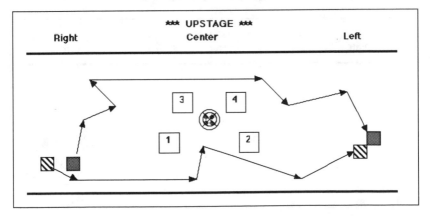

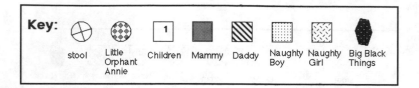

FIG.5: Naughty Girl enters from right and crosses to down left, laughing and taunting.

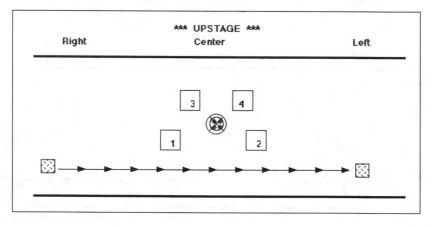

FIG.6: Two Big Black Things enter from left and whisk Naughty Girl offstage left.

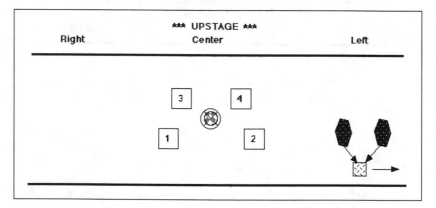

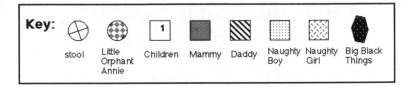

Key: stool | Little Orphant Annie | Children | Mammy | Daddy | Naughty Boy | Naughty Girl | Big Black Things

FIG.7: Children and Annie stand in a line and face audience.

*** UPSTAGE ***

Right   Center   Left

⊗

| 1 | 3 | ◈ | 4 | 2 |

How the People Got Fire
by L.E. McCullough

originally published in *Plays of America for Children*,
Smith & Kraus, 1996

How the People Got Fire is based on a tale from the Maidu tribe of Central California. The Maidu flourished in the coastal country and central valleys north of modern-day San Francisco. They resided in houses made of large earth mounds and lived largely from the bounty of the lush land that surrounded them. The central motif of capturing fire from the gods and bringing it to earth in a flute is widespread in many cultures around the world, recalling the ancient Greek myth of Prometheus, who gave fire to the human race in defiance of the chief god Zeus. Native American tales about the creation of the world typically use animals as protagonists, emphasizing the human race's dependence upon nature for survival and the belief that animals have spirits that must be respected and honored.

TIME: The dawn of human history

PLACE: In the vast North American desert left by melting glaciers

CAST:

Narrator
Thunder (male)
Lightning (female)
Lizard
Lizard's Brother
Frog
Fox
Deer
Coyote
A Mother
The People (2-4 actors)
3 Daughters of Thunder & Lightning

Woswosim — big bird, ally of Thunder & Lightning
Toyeskom — small bird, ally of The People
Skunk
Dog
Gopher
Wildcat
Chipmunk
Mouse
A Child
(Narrator lines can be given to more than one actor)

STAGE SET: arrayed upstage from right to left are some medium-sized boulders (painted styrofoam, cardboard); one boulder is at down right; at mid center there is a circular campfire made of stones and some kindling sticks; at mid left four corncobs are arranged in a pile

PROPS: a dozen orange-painted small blocks to denote embers; a flute (or tinwhistle or recorder would be easier to carry); an apron; four corncobs; a spear or club

SPECIAL EFFECTS: thunder, lightning, rain and wind sounds; lightning flashes

MUSIC: *Song of the Embers* played by flute (or tinwhistle or recorder)

COSTUMES: all characters can dress in simple one-piece, one-color smocks and sandals; animal masks and headdresses can be made for animal characters; bird characters Woswosim and Toyeskom can be adorned with feathers, Thunder and Lightning and their Three Daughters with raincloud and lightning symbols (the daughters also wear aprons); faces of Narrator and The People can be painted with simple designs based on Native American symbols

FIG.1: Basic stage plan; opening setting.

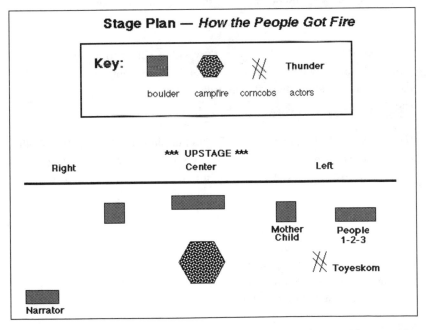

(FIG. 1) STAGE IS DARK. LIGHTS UP SLOWLY STAGE RIGHT, where Narrator sits on a rock. He speaks to the audience:

NARRATOR
A long time ago, there was no fire in the world.

The **Narrator's** voice is somber; this is a serious situation, and the audience does not know if it will turn out happily.

*LIGHTS UP STAGE LEFT on **The People** (including **Mother** and **Child**) sitting on the ground, huddled in a circle, shivering.*

Mother consoles **Child**, patting **Child's** hair as **Child** huddles forlornly.

NARRATOR
The People who lived in the world then had heard of fire, and they wanted it to keep warm and to cook their food. They had a bird, a small bird named Toyeskom, who had a very bright red eye.

Narrator points to left as **Toyeskom** enters.

Toyeskom enters from left and is greeted enthusiastically by The People.

Toyeskom dances onstage as **The People** stand and clap and shout.

TOYESKOM
I am Toyeskom, my eye is bright and red; with its shiny glare, I help The People to be fed!

Toyeskom points to his eye, then stretches arms outward in a beneficient manner.

The People guide Toyeskom to a spot on the ground a mid left where four corncobs have been piled.

The People stand behind **Toyeskom** and point to the corncobs, begging him to stare at the corncobs with his red eye.

NARRATOR
When The People wanted their food cooked, they had Toyeskom turn his bright red eye toward the food, and he would stare at it for a

long time. The stare from his bright red eye would make the food warm and cook it.

*Toyeskom kneels, cocks his head toward the corncobs, shakes and bobs head as if his motions are cooking the food. A **Child** steps forward and addresses its **Mother**.*

The People rub their hands and stomachs, anticipating the cooked food.

NARRATOR
But it took a really long time.

CHILD
Mommy, I am sooooo hungry! When are we ever going to eat?

MOTHER
Patience, my child. Our meal will be cooked in only another few hours.

PEOPLE
(chanting) We are The People! We must find fire! We are The People! We must find fire! We are The People! We must find fire!

The People chant and stamp their feet, raise their fists in the air.

Toyeskom finishes cooking, rises and hands corncobs to People, who graciously thank him; he exits left.

The People take corncobs, bow to **Toyeskom,** and retire to behind the boulders as he exits.

*(FIG. 2) LIGHTS DIM ON PEO-PLE; LIGHTS UP STAGE RIGHT on **Thunder** and **Lightning** who enter from right, arms upraised, and stand at right of campfire.*

Thunder and **Lightning** enter with great aplomb and dignity.

FIG.2: *Thunder and Lightning enter and dance to down center;
their Three Daughters enter, pick up embers from fire and sit;
Mother, Child, and The People move behind boulders at up left.*

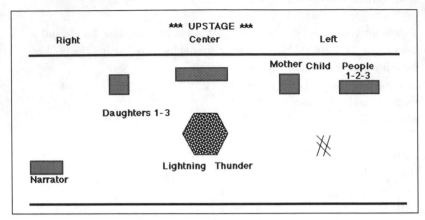

NARRATOR

In truth, there was fire in the world, but only Thunder and Lightning, who were married to each other, had it. And they would let no one else have any.

Thunder and Lightning dance and twirl to center stage; they drop several fire embers into center of campfire and fall back as fire blazes up.

THUNDER

I am Thunder, Lord of the World! When I speak my mind, The People tremble and fear!

LIGHTNING

I am Lightning, Thunder's Elegant Queen! When I dance through the heavens, my feet paint the evening sky!

Thunder and **Lightning** pull embers from a pocket of their costumes and drop them into the fire. They stand at down center and address audience in a haughty, fearsome tone.

Thunder & Lightning's Three Daughters enter from right; they each pick up an ember from the fire and put it in their aprons, guarding them carefully.

Three Daughters come onstage with more delicacy than their parents and gently pick up embers and place them in aprons.

NARRATOR
Thunder and Lightning had Three Daughters, who kept bits of fire in their aprons, so they would always have plenty.

Three Daughters scurry behind Thunder and Lightning and sit; LIGHTS DIM TO HALF and **Woswosim** *enters from stage right, dancing toward campfire. He carries a spear or club, with which he slashes the air and fends off imaginary foes.*

Woswosim enters warily, as if awaiting attack.

NARRATOR
And at night, when darkness fell, a huge giant bird — Woswosim — guarded the main fire and made sure no one got near to it.

Woswosim stands with weapon at ready, sternly facing audience.

(FIG. 3) At down center **Woswosim** *stands guard over fire as Thunder, Lightning, and their Three Daughters retire to stage right, lie down, and sleep. LIGHTS OUT, THEN UP STAGE LEFT.* **Lizard** *and* **Lizard's Brother** *crawl on from left, lazily leaning on elbows at down left.*

Lizard and **Lizard's Brother** yawn, stretch, roll on ground; they are a bit silly and slapstick.

FIG.3: Thunder, Lightning, Three Daughters sleep upstage right as Woswosim guards fire at down center; Lizard and Lizard's Brother enter from left and laze around at down left.

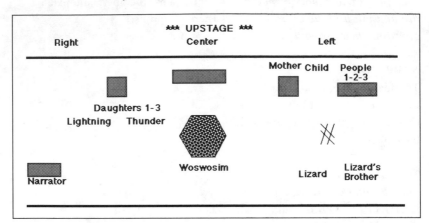

NARRATOR
One morning Lizard and his brother were sitting on a rock, sunning themselves. Lizard looked west and was amazed at what he saw.

LIZARD
Brother, look! Over there to the west! What do you see? *(points right toward campfire)*

Lizard rises to knees and points.

LIZARD'S BROTHER
I see. . . I see. . . I see smoke!

Lizard's Brother peers intently, rises to knees.

LIZARD
And?

LIZARD'S BROTHER
And where there is smoke. . .

126 Part Eight

LIZARD
Yes?

LIZARD'S BROTHER
There is. . . there is. . . there is
fire!

LIZARD
Yes! Yes! Yes!

They hug each other happily;
Coyote enters from stage left.

NARRATOR
Lizard and his brother ran back
home. On the way they saw
Coyote.

Coyote enters upright, sniffing in the
air.

Lizard and Lizard's Brother stand
and run to Coyote.

LIZARD & LIZARD'S BROTHER
Coyote! Coyote! Guess what we
have seen?

COYOTE
Oh, it's you lizards again! What is
it *this* time?

Coyote acts snobbish and uninter-
ested.

LIZARD
We have seen fire!

COYOTE
Fire?

LIZARD'S BROTHER
Just a little smoke, actually.

LIZARD
But where there is smoke—

LIZARD'S BROTHER
There is fire!

Lizard and his brother jump up and down excitedly, but Coyote is unimpressed.

COYOTE
Listen, Coyote is the Trickster around here. *I* am the one who makes up jokes and pranks. You can't kid a kidder. Smoke! Fire! I don't believe a word you lizards say!

LIZARD & LIZARD'S BROTHER
(they point right) Look!

Coyote turns, sees smoke, and is startled.

COYOTE
It *is* smoke! It comes from the land where Thunder and Lightning live. Quick, lizards, we must call the other animals at once! *(turns and looks stage left to where The People sit huddled)* We must get fire to The People.

LIZARD & LIZARD'S BROTHER
Calling all animals! Calling all animals! Come meet with Coyote at once!

Coyote points to **The People**.

Lizard and **Lizard's Brother** walk up and down left side of stage, shouting. **Frog** hops and sticks out tongue, **Fox** darts about, **Snake** makes slithering motions with arms, **Wildcat** growls and claws at air, **Mouse** scurries, **Deer** walks with head up high and very alert, **Dog** shakes itself and barks, **Chipmunk** enters timidly, **Skunk** waddles on, nose down and sniffing.

FIG.4: Coyote and other animals (Frog, Fox, Snake, Wildcat, Mouse, Deer, Dog, Chipmunk, Skunk) enter from left and confer.

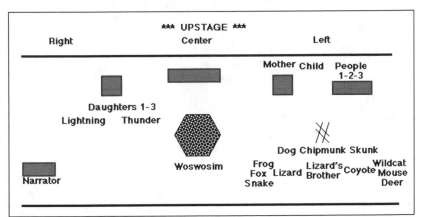

(FIG. 4) **Frog, Fox, Snake, Wildcat, Mouse, Deer, Dog, Chipmunk** and **Skunk** *enter from stage left as their names are called, dancing briefly or miming their animal gaits before gathering around Coyote and Lizard and Lizard's Brother.*

NARRATOR
And in awhile, all the animals of the World came: Frog. . . Fox. . . Snake. . . Wildcat. . . Mouse. . . Deer. . . Dog. . . Chipmunk. . . Skunk.

Animals listen attentively.

COYOTE
Animals of the World, we have seen smoke!

Animals gasp in disbelief.

LIZARD
And where there is smoke—

LIZARD'S BROTHER
There is fire!

ANIMALS
(cheer) Hurrah! They have seen smoke! They have seen fire!

COYOTE
Quiet, please. This smoke and fire belong to Thunder and Lightning.

ANIMALS
(moan) Oh, no. . . not Thunder and Lightning!

MOUSE
We must get this fire and bring it to The People.

FROG
That will not be easy. They say an evil bird, Woswosim, guards the fire at night. He never sleeps.

WILDCAT
That is no problem. *(mimes motions)* I, Wildcat, will creep up on this evil bird and devour him before he has time to say "one, two, three"!

DEER
The noise would wake Thunder and Lightning and their Three Daughters. You would never come back alive.

SNAKE
Wait! How about if *I* sneak up and bite this Woswoswim in the ankle?

DOG
You would be crushed when he fell on you. You would never bring fire back.

CHIPMUNK
I know! I will face this giant bird.

FOX
You? You're a little teeny chipmunk!

CHIPMUNK
I *know* what I am, Fox! I am a chipmunk — a chipmunk who plays the *flute.*

Chipmunk takes out a flute and plays a sweet melody; animals sigh and swoon. **Sound cue:** *first two bars of "Song of the Embers."*

SKUNK
That is truly beautiful. Chipmunk can play his flute and make Woswosim fall asleep. That will give us a chance to take the fire.

Animals mutter their assent; LIGHTS DIM, A FEW SECONDS PAUSE, THEN UP TO HALF STAGE RIGHT where Thunder and Lightning and their Three Daughters are asleep in the corner. Woswosim stands in front of campfire, spreading his wings and pacing slowly to and fro.

Frog, Fox, Snake, Wildcat, Skunk, Lizard and **Lizard's Brother** shrink back toward down left and crouch, huddled together and "shh-shh"-ing each other. **Mouse, Dog, Chipmunk, Coyote,** and **Deer** creep single file behind campfire.

WOSWOSIM

I, giant Woswosim, am the fiercest bird in the sky! I am so strong that I never sleep! Only babies sleep! I never sleep, and no one in the world can defeat me!

*(FIG. 5) Chipmunk, Mouse, Dog, Coyote, and Deer have crept toward campfire, crouched low or laying on the ground while other animals remain at down left. Chipmunk takes out his flute and begins to play softly. **Sound cue:** "Song of the Embers."*

FIG.5: Chipmunk, Mouse, Dog, Coyote, and Deer creep toward campfire while other animals remain at down left.

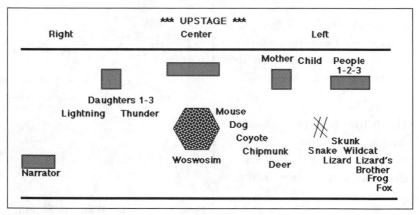

WOSWOSIM

(jumps up, alert) What sound is that? Who disturbs the campfire of Thunder and Lightning?

Chipmunk stops; other animals
shrink back. After a pause,
Chipmunk plays again.

WOSWOSIM
(relaxes) Hmmm. Must be some
kind of bird. A night bird like me.
Well, you can't have too many *me*
around the world.

As the music continues,
Woswosim sits in front of camp-
fire and nods his head.

WOSWOSIM
(yawns) That is a very pretty
melody. *(yawns)* So very...very...
very...*(falls asleep)*

(FIG. 6) Chipmunk stops playing;
other animals enter campsite as
described below.

FIG.6: *Mouse takes fire from Daughters' aprons and gives it to Dog,*
Coyote and puts it in Chipmunk's flute, who gives it to Deer.

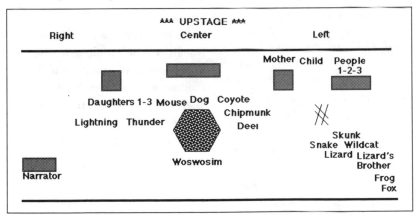

NARRATOR

When the animals saw that Woswosim had fallen asleep, they sprang into action. Mouse untied the Three Daughters' aprons and took their fire. He put some fire in Dog's ear, some in Coyote's mouth, and the rest in the flute. He gave the flute to Deer, being the swiftest runner. But then, all of a sudden, Thunder and Lightning awoke.

THUNDER

What is going on?

LIGHTNING

Who are all these animals?

THREE DAUGHTERS

Our aprons are untied! They've stolen our fire!

THUNDER

They've stolen all the fire! Thieves!

LIGHTNING

Woswosim, wake up! After them!

*(FIG. 7) The animals scatter across stage, ducking and covering, guarding their fire; Woswosim stands in campfire, flapping his wings; Thunder and Lightning and their Three Daughters begin dancing, creating big rainstorms with wind and hail and terrible lightning. **Sound cue:** thunder, lightning, rain, and wind sounds. **Light effects:** lightning flashes.*

Thunder, **Lightning** and **Three Daughters** sit upright.

Thunder, **Lightning** and **Three Daughters** rise and jump in place; **Woswosim** leaps into the middle of the campfire and flaps his wings angrily. **Thunder, Lightning,** and **Three Daughters** begin dancing, raising arms skyward and wailing.

FIG.7: Spirits awake and dance storms on animals fleeing to left;
Woswosim jumps in campfire; Skunk moves toward center.

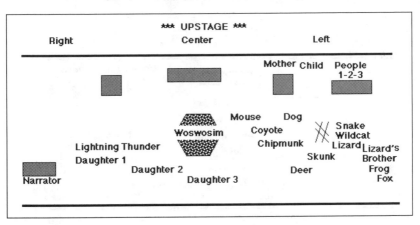

NARRATOR

Thunder and Lightning gave chase.
They danced and danced in the
sky and made big winds and rainstorms that shook the world, from
one end to the other.

Chipmunk, Mouse, Dog, Coyote
and Deer reel and tumble, strug-
gle to get up; Thunder, Lightning,
Three Daughters, and Woswosim
stalk them.

Thunder and Lightning run first to
back of campfire, then retrace steps
and run to down center as Three
Daughters continue to dance.
Chipmunk, Mouse, Dog, Coyote,
and Deer reel and fall as other
Animals cheer them on, trying to get
them to safety at down left.
Chipmunk, Mouse, Dog, Coyote,
and Deer lay in a heap at center just
to left of campfire as Thunder,
Lightning, and Three Daughters
stand threateningly over them.

NARRATOR

But just as Thunder and Lightning and
their Three Daughters were about
to catch up with the animals…
Skunk rushed in to the fray.

Meanwhile, Skunk has edged closer
to center stage and jumps between
Chipmunk, Mouse, Dog, Coyote,
and Deer and the angry Spirits.

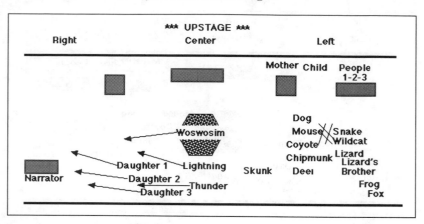

(FIG. 8) Skunk jumps between animals and pursuers; facing Thunder and Lightning, he throws forth his arms as if casting a net.

NARRATOR

And he sent toward them a mighty blast of his own wind. . . a powerful wind all skunks command even to this day, when they battle a bigger foe.

With his hands, **Skunk** "throws" his wind at the **Spirits**, who shout and recoil instantly, falling to ground and kneeling and groveling as they hold their noses.

Thunder, Lightning, Three Daughters, and Woswosim fall down, shrink back, coughing and rubbing their eyes.

THUNDER & LIGHTNING

Stop! Stop! No more, skunk! Stop! This wind is killing us!

SKUNK

I will stop. But only if you promise that after today, you must never try to take fire from The People.

THUNDER & LIGHTNING
(groveling) We promise! We promise!

SKUNK

I accept your promise and your word you will keep it. Forever more, you must stay up in the sky and be thunder and be lightning. That is where you must be.

Skunk points to sky.

Thunder and Lightning and their Three Daughters and Woswosim mumble and shake their heads in assent, exiting slowly right. LIGHTS UP LEFT on The People, standing now, looking up and excitedly pointing at the sky.

As the **Spirits** exit, Skunk mimes "bringing back" his wind with gathering motions. **The People** rise and emerge from behind boulders, and the **Animals** converge around the corncob site at mid left, which will now become the new campfire for **The People**.

NARRATOR

And so the animals returned to the world with fire, which they gave to The People.

(FIG. 9) Animals hand fire embers to The People; The People thank them profusely. The Animals creep, crawl, scamper, and bound offstage left.

FIG.9: *Animals hand fire embers to The People, then creep, crawl, scamper, and bound offstage left.*

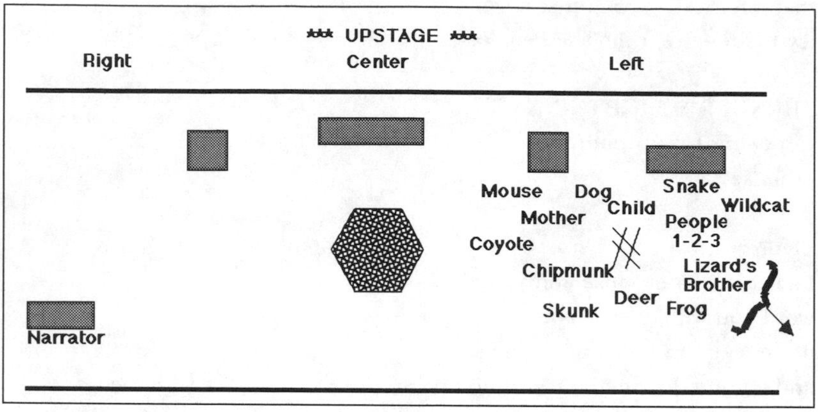

(FIG. 10) *The People place embers into their new campfire, then gather in a semicircle round the fire and sit, holding hands and staring into their new campfire as LIGHTS DIM.*

NARRATOR
And The People have had it ever since.

LIGHTS OUT. **Sound cue:** *"Song of the Embers."*

THE END.

As LIGHTS DIM, **The People** bow their heads.

FIG.10: The People gather in a semicircle around their new fire and sit, holding hands, and staring into their new campfire as lights dim.

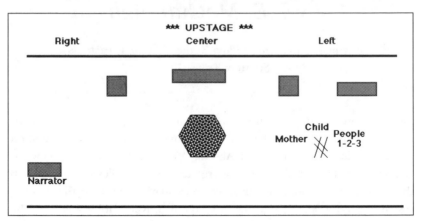

Song of the Embers

by L.E. McCullough

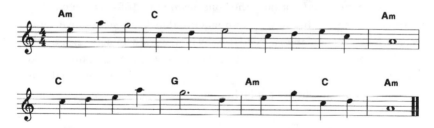

The Story of *Silent Night*
by L.E. McCullough

originally published in *Plays of the Songs of Christmas*,
Smith & Kraus, 1996

Almost as interesting as the circumstances surrounding the creation of *Silent Night* by Franz Gruber, is the trail of the song's subsequent dissemination into the world beyond Oberndorf, Austria. After its premiere performance at Midnight Mass in 1818, the song was forgotten until the following spring when the manuscript was discovered by the repairman who came to fix the church's rusted organ. He sang the untitled song on his travels until it was heard by two professional folk-singing families, the Rainers and the Strassers, who each made what had come to be called *The Song from Heaven* part of their regular repertoire. In 1834 the Strassers sang the song for the King of Prussia, who liked it so much he ordered it sung by his own choir every Christmas Eve. The Rainers first sang the song in the United States in 1839 in New York City. Franz Gruber did not hear the song again until 1854; he shocked the music authorities of the day by announcing that he, a small-town music teacher, had composed the music to this, by now, world-famous song. Fr. Mohr died in 1848 without ever knowing the song had been sung again. In 1863 *Stille Nacht! Heilige Nacht!* was translated into English by Reverend John Freedman Young, the Episcopal bishop of Florida.

TIME: Christmas Eve, 1818

PLACE: Church of St. Nicholas, Oberndorf, Austria

CAST:

	Fr. Josef Mohr	Sexton Sirker
	Franz Gruber	Altar Boy
	Herr Hummel	Guitar Student (Anna)
	Frau Schmidt	Congregation Members
	Choir Members	

STAGE SET: church interior with altar and 2 pews (or benches); Gruber's music studio with table and 2 chairs

PROPS: Psalm book; baton; shovel; guitar; music paper; quill pen; ink pot

MUSIC: *Silent Night*

COSTUMES: characters dress in early 19th-century German peasant garb; Fr. Mohr wears standard black cassock and a wide-brimmed hat, for Mass he wears a chasuble — a white blouse over his cassock; Herr Hummel could wear fancy frock coat and breeches; Gruber and other men wear more common vests, trousers, and boots; women wear plain dresses and bonnets

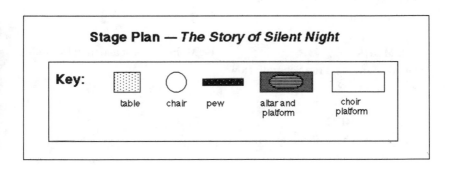

FIG.1. *Basic stage plan; opening setting.*

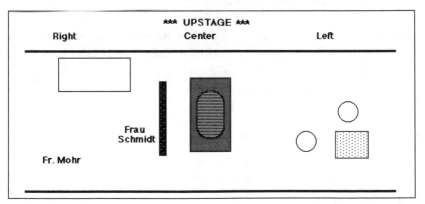

*(FIG. 1) LIGHTS UP RIGHT AND CENTER ON CHURCH INTERIOR. An old woman, **Frau Schmidt**, kneels in a pew, head bowed and hands folded in prayer.*

FRAU SCHMIDT
And please, oh Lord, a special prayer for those in our village suffering from hunger and hardship this Christmas Eve.

Frau Schmidt is feeble, with great worry in her voice.

*(She blesses herself, rises and turns to exit right as **Fr. Josef Mohr** enters from right, blessing himself; he carries a Psalm book.)*

FR. MOHR
Good afternoon, Frau Schmidt. How are you today?

Fr. Mohr is robust and friendly, smiling.

FRAU SCHMIDT
I am in good health, Father. Though my cottage may be washed away with all this rain and melting snow.

FR. MOHR
It has been raining quite a bit lately.

FRAU SCHMIDT
Six weeks, Father. Six weeks it has either rained or snowed every day. Is God trying to drown us? Have we people of Oberndorf so offended him that he is going to flood our sins away?

Frau Schmidt looks around and at sky, as if she fears the church roof might collapse.

FR. MOHR
(chuckles) I do not know if it is time yet to build an ark, Frau Schmidt. But you may be right about God

sending us a message. He is always speaking to us, even in the most humble ways. We must train ourselves to listen.

FRAU SCHMIDT
Yes, Father. Good day. *(blesses herself, exits right)*

FR. MOHR
Good day. And keep dry.

Fr. Mohr blesses the departing **Frau Schmidt** with a sign of the Cross, sighs.

(FIG. 2) Fr. Mohr crosses to altar platform, where he kneels and prays.

FIG.2: Fr. Mohr kneels at altar; Herr Hummel enters excitedly from right, followed later by Sexton Sirker.

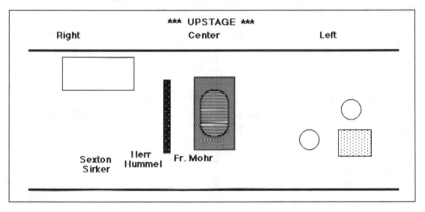

FR. MOHR
Dear God, I ask that you not only hear our prayers, but open our ears to hear your voice as well. Open our ears to the needs of our fellow men and women. Open our ears to the sounds of music and laughter celebrating the birthday of your only

Fr. Mohr faces left so his words can be heard by audience; he speaks with head uplifted.

son, Jesus. And open our ears…to the silence…yes, the silence…so we can better hear the sound of your divine, majestic voice as it speaks to us through the world you have created for us to enjoy.

Herr Hummel enters excitedly from right, waving a baton, and crosses to center.

HERR HUMMEL
Father Mohr! Father Mohr!

Herr Hummel halts at pew and stands to right of Fr. Mohr, who stands and turns to face him. **Herr Hummel** is beside himself with distress.

FR. MOHR
(stands) Yes, Herr Hummel?

HERR HUMMEL
Father, the organ is ruined!

FR. MOHR
Ruined?

HERR HUMMEL
The dampness from this rain has rusted the pipes. The pedals are stuck. And the bellows have been nibbled by mice. The entire instrument is ruined!

Herr Hummel taps the air with his baton to emphasize each disaster.

FR. MOHR
Is it beyond repair?

HERR HUMMEL
I don't know about that. But for mass tonight, there will be no organ.

FR. MOHR
And without the organ, there will be no choir.

HERR HUMMEL
No choir, no music. And how can there *not* be music for Midnight Mass at St. Nicholas Church?

Sexton Sirker rushes in from right, carrying a muddy shovel.

FR. MOHR
Sexton Sirker! You look exhausted!

SEXTON SIRKER
Bad news, Father! The river has run over its banks. I have been digging since daybreak to keep it out, but water is flowing under the church.

Sexton Sirker leans on the shovel and wipes his brow.

FR. MOHR
Will it get worse?

SEXTON SIRKER
In a few hours the entire building could tear away from the foundation — and collapse!

HERR HUMMEL
Ach! We have no organ, no choir, and now no church!

SEXTON SIRKER
What shall we do, Father?

FR. MOHR

(holds up the Psalm book, reflects for a moment) "I will sing a new song to you, O God; upon a ten-stringed harp I will play to you." *(pause)* There is nothing we can do about the river, gentlemen. But there *is* something we can do about the music. Meet me here at nine o'clock — with the choir.

LIGHTS OUT. Sirker and Hummel exit right. Fr. Mohr crosses to mid center to left of altar.

*(FIG. 3) LIGHTS UP LEFT ON MUSIC STUDIO where **Franz Gruber** sits teaching a **Guitar Student** who holds a guitar. Some music paper and a quill pen and ink pot are on the table. Fr. Mohr stands to their right behind Gruber.*

Fr. Mohr turns to face audience. **Sexton Sirker** and **Herr Hummel** look quizzically at each other, shrug their shoulders and turn to exit right.

Franz Gruber faces audience and leans forward to better hear the **Guitar Student**, who faces left and plays a final G chord.

FIG.3: Fr. Mohr watches Franz Gruber teach a Guitar Student.

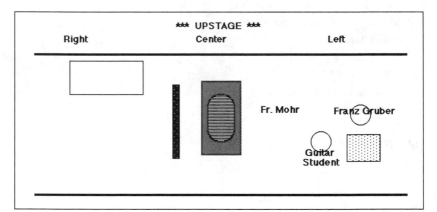

FRANZ GRUBER
Very good, Anna. The Bach minuet in G is a difficult piece to interpret with proper feeling. You are well on your way to mastering it.

Franz Gruber is very scholarly, precise, and correct in manner.

GUITAR STUDENT
Thank you, Herr Gruber. *(notices Fr. Mohr)* Father Mohr!

Guitar Student looks to her left and sees **Fr. Mohr**.

Gruber and the Guitar Student stand.

FR. MOHR
Please, please, I do not wish to disturb your lesson.

Franz Gruber bows his head; **Guitar Student** curtsies.

FRANZ GRUBER
A visit from you is an honor, not a disturbance. Come, enter.

Gruber offers his chair to Fr. Mohr, who sits; Guitar Student sits.

FR. MOHR
Herr Gruber, the organ at St. Nicholas has been ruined by the damp. Herr Hummel cannot play his Christmas music for the Midnight Mass.

Franz Gruber stands to the left of **Fr. Mohr** and faces the audience.

FRANZ GRUBER
That is a tragedy. Herr Hummel is a fine organist.

FR. MOHR
And you are a fine guitarist.

FRANZ GRUBER
(*chuckles*) You are too kind, Father.
I am an untrained musician. I play
nothing of significance — only a few
folk tunes.

FR. MOHR
Like that minuet by the folk musician Johann Sebastian Bach? (*pauses
as Franz Gruber chuckles*) Herr
Gruber, you are much too modest.
Of course, the instrument you play —
the guitar — is not used in the
church.

Franz Gruber walks to down left, still
facing the audience.

FRANZ GRUBER
(*bitterly*) "Too common," say the
authorities. "A peasant instrument."
Not "noble enough" for serious wor-
ship.

FR. MOHR
When the humblest peasant speaks
with the voice of God, he is as noble
as any duke or prince. Herr Gruber,
I need you — and your guitar — to
perform music at Midnight Mass.

Franz Gruber turns to Fr. Mohr.

FRANZ GRUBER
Midnight Mass!

FR. MOHR
We must compose a song for the
choir. This afternoon.

Fr. Mohr leans forward, hands pleading.

FRANZ GRUBER
Impossible!

Franz Gruber steps back, half turns
away from Fr. Mohr. As he considers the
priest's request, he looks to his left or
out toward the audience, above their
heads as if looking deep into his own soul.

FR. MOHR
It is your chance to make music that
is truly divine.

*Gruber says nothing for a moment,
then takes the guitar from Guitar
Student; Fr. Mohr rises and directs
Guitar Student to sit in his chair as
Franz Gruber sits in the front chair
facing audience.*

FRANZ GRUBER
Anna, take pen and paper. You will
be our scribe.

*Anna pulls her chair to table and
readies herself to write.*

FRANZ GRUBER
Have you any verses, Father?

FR. MOHR
I am afraid my desperation has not
produced inspiration. Have you a
melody?

FRANZ GRUBER
I cannot write a melody without a
picture.

FR. MOHR
A picture?

FRANZ GRUBER
A picture in my mind. If I write a song
about a person, I must see that person. A house, I must see that house.
A Savior… *(shrugs)* I have never
seen a Savior, Father. Have you?

Franz Gruber uses his hand to outline
a picture frame.

Fr. Mohr nods "no" and paces to and fro. Franz Gruber stares away toward audience. No one speaks for several seconds.

Guitar Student looks back and forth between Fr. Mohr and Franz Gruber.

FRANZ GRUBER
Listen to that rain. It is so persistent.

FR. MOHR
(stops pacing) Yet so gentle. Almost like a lullaby.

FRANZ GRUBER
Yes, a lullaby. A mother and her child. Asleep in the still of the night.

FR. MOHR
Surrounded only by silence. The silence of peace.

FRANZ GRUBER
Can you imagine that holy night in Bethlehem? How quiet it must have been after the Christ child was born!

GUITAR STUDENT
They say not even the animals made a sound.

FRANZ GRUBER
Yes, in the stable! In the moonlight flooding down upon the stable.

Franz Gruber's voice gets more excited as his "picture" becomes more clear. He and Fr. Mohr stare down center at the same imaginary image.

FR. MOHR
All is calm. All is bright.

FRANZ GRUBER
Shepherds and animals gathered around the Virgin Mother and her child.

FR. MOHR
Holy infant. So tender.

GUITAR STUDENT
So mild.

Guitar Student also stares at down center.

FRANZ GRUBER
Sleeping. . . sleeping. . .

FR. MOHR
In heavenly peace.

Allow a second or two after this line for the sense of "heavenly peace" to settle in. Suddenly, **Franz Gruber** breaks the spell, turns to the guitar student in a burst of animation and resolve.

FRANZ GRUBER
Anna, take down this melody...a lullaby...not too fast...three-four time...

Franz Gruber begins playing first few notes of "Silent Night". LIGHTS OUT FOR TEN SECONDS, THEN UP RIGHT AND CENTER ON CHURCH where **The Congregation** *is gathered for Midnight Mass.*

(FIG. 4) **The Choir** *stands against back curtain with Franz Gruber and his guitar to their right, Herr Hummel and his baton in front; Frau Schmidt and Anna sit in the pew as other members of The Congregation stand behind altar; Fr. Mohr and* **An Altar Boy** *are at the altar facing right.*

FIG.4: Setting for Midnight Mass.

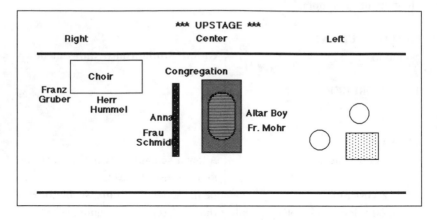

FR. MOHR

My friends, this is a troublesome time in the world. A troublesome time in Austria. A troublesome time in our own small village of Oberndorf. But we must not fall victim to fear. For fear is a temptation to sin. Instead, let us remember words from today's gospel: "And the angel said to them, 'Do not be afraid, for behold, I bring you good news of great joy which shall be to all the people. For today in the town of David, a Savior has been born to you who is Christ the Lord. And this shall be a sign to you: you will find an Infant wrapped in swaddling clothes and lying in a manger.'" Let us raise our voices in song, and sing of this good news.

(He points to Herr Hummel, who cues Franz Gruber to begin playing guitar; Choir sings "Silent Night".)

Fr. Mohr addresses Congregation but occasionally speaks toward audience.

Congregation members bless themselves, bow heads, raise hands to sky as they silently pray.

CHOIR *(sing)*
Silent night, holy night
All is calm, all is bright
Round yon Virgin Mother and child
Holy Infant so tender and mild
Sleep in heavenly peace
Sleep in heavenly peace

Choir is joined by Congregation.

CHOIR & CONGREGATION *(sing)*
Silent night, holy night
Shepherds quake at the sight
Glories stream from heaven afar
Heavenly hosts sing alleluia
Christ the Savior is born
Christ the Savior is born

Sexton Sirker bursts in from right.

SEXTON SIRKER
The river! The river! It has gone
down!

*Congregation sighs, exclaims with
relief and joy.*

ANNA
The town is saved!

Anna stands.

FRAU SCHMIDT
It is a miracle! God has heard our
prayers!

Frau Schmidt, still kneeling, clutches
Anna with joy.

FR. MOHR
Now let Him hear our thanks! *(turns
to audience)* Everyone! Lift up your
voice in thanks!

Fr. Mohr steps to down center and
encourages audience to sing.

ALL *(sing)*
Silent night, holy night
Son of God, love's pure light

Radiant beams from Thy holy face
With the dawn of redeeming grace
Jesus, Lord, at Thy birth
Jesus, Lord, at Thy birth

Silent night, holy night
All is calm, all is bright
Round yon Virgin Mother and child
Holy Infant so tender and mild
Sleep in heavenly peace
Sleep in heavenly peace

LIGHTS OUT.

THE END.

Silent Night

(Words: Joseph Mohr / Music: Franz Gruber / Arranged: L.E. McCullough)

— GLOSSARY —

acting area. The space in which the actors move while onstage during the play. (Fig. 8)

actors. The persons who perform the roles designated in the script.

antagonist. The character of a play who attempts to prevent the protagonist from achieving his or her goal.

apron. The part of the stage in front that extends beyond the proscenium into the audience. (Fig. 9)

arena stage. A type of stage where the audience totally encircles the stage; also called *theatre-in-the-round*. (Fig. 10)

assistant stage manager. The person who helps the stage manager and keeps notes of what goes on during rehearsal, especially any changes in the script.

audience area. The area of the theatre where the audience is seated to watch the play. (Fig. 8)

audition. An interview held by the director to appraise an actor's suitability for a role when casting a play.

backcloth. A piece of canvas or sheet painted to depict a scene and hung at the rear of the stage by a batten. (see **drop**, Fig. 23)

backstage area. The area of offstage space in which actors enter and exit from the stage, where costume changes occur, where scenery and props are stored.

batten. A horizontal pipe, bar, or wood strip attached to the ceiling and from which pieces of scenery or lighting can be hung. (Fig. 23)

beamlight. A parabolic light that has no lens, typically used to cast a narrow beam that simulates moon or sun spots.

blocking. The process whereby a director shows actors where and how to move during the play.

booth (light or sound). A small, often enclosed space set above the stage, usually in the rear of the theatre, from which light and sound equipment is operated. (see **tech table**)

box office manager. The person who sells tickets to the play.

box set. A type of set that has tall flats enclosing the stage on three sides. (Fig. 24)

break a leg! A traditional theatre expression said to actors before a performance, meaning to "do well and have a good show."

business. The physical activities, aside from entering, exiting, and crossing the stage, that an actor performs, usually with a prop, to emphasize the realism of the character. **Necessary business** comes naturally from the scripted action of the play: riding a horse, killing a dragon, playing the piano, etc. **Imposed business** is what an actor does to enhance the nature of the character or add an element of interpretation to the story line: adjusting the horse's saddle before mounting the horse, polishing the spear before killing the dragon, sipping from a coffee cup while playing the piano.

cast. The collective name for the actors in a play.

cast call. The exact time when actors are supposed to appear at the theatre to prepare for a rehearsal or performance.

casting. The process by which the director auditions and selects the actors for a play.

climax. An event in a play that leads to the resolution; the highest point of dramatic conflict and excitement.

conflict. The opposition of wills and forces between the protagonist and antagonist; the conflict is the central problem that creates the play's dramatic tension.

contact sheet. A sheet with the names, phone numbers, and addresses of actors, crew, and parents involved in the play production.

corner stage. A type of three-sided stage set into the corner of a room. (Fig. 11)

costume chart. A chart made and kept by the costumer that tells exactly what clothing and accessories are needed for each character. (Fig. 31)

costume parade. The segment of dress rehearsal when actors walk in full costume under the stage lights to make sure everything that needs to be seen is seen and everything that shouldn't be seen isn't.

costumer. The person who assembles (quite often sews) the actors' costumes (clothes, wigs, masks), fitting and dressing them for performance.

crew call. The exact time when crew members are supoposed to appear at the theatre to prepare for a rehearsal or performance.

curtain. A drape or hanging screen at the front of the stage that opens in the middle and can be drawn back and forth to shield the entire stage from audience view; also, a term used to signify the end of the play.

curtain call. The reappearance of all the actors at the end of the show to accept the audience's applause.

cut-out. A piece of scenery cut out of cardboard or wood to represent bushes, trees, rocks, buildings, mountains, or other landscape. (see **ground row**)

cyclorama. A large curved background piece encircling most of the stage and used to suggest a panoramic landscape or sky. (Fig. 26)

dialogue. A point in a play where two characters are speaking to each other; generally used to mean all the spoken lines of a play.

director. The person who works with the actors and stage crew to interpret the play and bring it from printed page to live performance.

director's notes. The observations the director makes on the execution of acting and technical cues during rehearsals and performances that are then read to the cast and crew.

drape. A curtain that prevents the audience from seeing the back or side walls of the stage. (Fig. 20)

dress rehearsal. The performance of the play with all elements in place — except the audience. Usually held the night before the play's public opening, a dress rehearsal has actors dressed in full costume and makeup and all technical cues ready to roll.

dresser. The person who helps actors with their costumes before and during the play.

drop. A piece of canvas or sheet painted to depict a scene and hung at the rear of the stage by a batten. (see **backcloth**, Fig. 23)

exterior set. A type of set that represents an outdoor location.

fill lighting. A type of lighting composition that uses light from behind, sides, or floor of the stage to supplement the main lights. (Fig. 36)

flat. A very lightweight wood frame covered with canvas that can easily be moved about to provide a scenic backdrop. (Fig. 20)

floodlight. A lighting instrument that gives a fixed spread of light.

follow spotlight. A spotlight that casts a variable beam that can be narrowed and widened by hand; it is generally used to follow actors around the stage. (Fig. 35)

frontcloth. A piece of canvas or sheet used at down left or right to hide a costume or scene change; it can also have scenery painted on it and function like a drop. (see **olio**, Fig. 23)

fourth wall. An imaginary wall that has been "removed" so that the audience can see what's going on in the room; some plays pretend this fourth wall is still intact and act as if the audience is nonexistent, while others assume the wall is gone and speak and act directly to the audience.

gel. A thin-sheeted colored filter that covers a light lens and reflects a colored light beam. (see **roundel**)

gobo. An aluminum sheet with cut-out pattern placed over a light lens to cast a simple pattern on the reflected beam.

greasepaint. A type of theatrical makeup foundation with an oil base.

ground row. A scenery piece set low on the ground along the front and sides of stage or in front of drops to suggest things like distant mountains, sea waves, fences, bushes, etc.; it can be made out of a flat, cardboard, wire, and so on and set to stand with braces at the back. (see **cut-out**)

house manager. The person who prepares the room for the audience:

setting up chairs (and removing them after the show), moving furniture, maintaining appropriate distance between stage and seats.

improvisation. A point in a play (or sometimes an entire play) where actors make up (or *ad-lib*) their actions and lines on the spot.

interior set. A type of set that represents an indoor location.

light cue chart. A chart made and kept by the lighting director that tells exactly what lights, light cues, and effects are needed and when. (Fig. 37)

lighting director. The person who operates the lights and creates lighting effects.

mailing flyer. A one-page announcement of a play that supplies information about the performance's What, When, Where, Who, and How Much. (Fig. 40)

makeup artist. The person who helps the actors design, apply, and remove makeup, hair dye, face paint, etc.

makeup chart. A chart made and kept by the makeup artist that tells exactly what makeup, wiggery, or hair styling are needed for each character.

monologue. A self-contained speech by one character.

multi-level stage. A type of stage that has two or more different levels that may be connected by ramps or steps. (Fig. 18)

news release. The mailing flyer in prose form, essentially a short feature article the publicity manager writes and sends to local print broadcast media. (Fig. 41)

olio. A piece of canvas or sheet piece used at down left or right to hide a costume or scene change; it can also have scenery painted on it and function like a drop. (see **frontcloth**, Fig. 23)

open the house. The command given by the house manager to admit the audience to the theatre, signifying that the pre-show preparations are complete.

pancake. A type of theatrical makeup foundation that is water-soluble.

permanent set. A set with two or more smaller sets that represent various separate locations.

places! The time call given by the stage manager that tells all actors and crew members to be in place ready to begin the play in a very few moments.

platform. A device for raising the stage up off the floor, a platform is a three-sided box made of a wooden frame and a flat solid top that is nailed, bolted, or screwed into the frame; a platform can be square or rectangular in shape or have wheels or casters attached to the bottom for mobility; also called a *rostrum*. (Figs. 14, 15, 16)

plot. The story line of a play that describes the characters and their actions.

pre-set. To set a prop or cue before the play begins, so it is ready to be used when needed.

producer. The person in charge of making the overall arrangements for organizing and presenting the play.

program chief. The person who puts together the program, selling ads if desired, and getting the program to the printers and back in time for the performance.

prompt script. A three-ring-binder copy of the script that is, in effect, the master version containing all dialogue, blocking, light, sound, and tech cues along with any other notes the director makes during rehearsals. (Fig. 39)

prompter. The person who stands offstage with a script and helps actors who may have forgotten their lines.

props. The objects on the stage that are not pieces of scenery or part of the stage architecture; there are **set props** whose function is to define and decorate the stage — tables, chairs, tombstones, campfires, hat racks, etc.; there are **hand props** — anything that is picked up or carried around the stage by actors during the course of the play, from forks to bazookas to marbles to dog leashes.

prop list. A list made and kept by the property master detailing all the props in a play. (Fig. 27)

prop table. The table where props are laid out backstage during rehearsals and performances.

property master. The person who maintains all the onstage properties (commonly called props) used by the actors or placed around the stage as part of the scenery.

proscenium. The arch that frames the stage opening. (Fig. 8)

proscenium stage. A type of stage setup that has the audience sitting in a single block in front of the stage facing the actors — as if the stage were a picture frame, where the audience "looks in" to the action. The front of a proscenium stage is marked by a curtain and an arch that supports it — this is the actual **proscenium**. (Fig. 8)

protagonist. The lead character of a play whose attempt to achieve a goal provides the play's main story.

PSA. Short for *public service announcement*, a brief, free announcement of an event on radio and television stations; a PSA is never more than 30 seconds in length. (Fig. 42)

publicity director. The person who handles publicity and advertising for the play.

raked stage. A type of stage that has an entire part of the stage sloping upward; to *rake* is to set the acting or audience area at an angle to the floor. (Fig. 19)

ramp. A sloped passageway onstage leading from a lower to a higher level. (Fig. 17)

Readers Theatre. A style of presenting literature — most often poems, short stories, novel excerpts, radio plays — as a staged play.

resolution. The conclusion of a play's plot; the point in the story line where the conflict reaches a climax, precipitates action, and results in a final determination of the characters' fates.

revolving stage. A type of stage in which the stage and scenery are mounted on a revolving carousel, with different sets (usually just two but possibly more) on different sides of the circle. (Fig. 13)

roundel. A circular piece of colored glass that covers a light lens and reflects a colored light beam. (see **gel**)

run. As a verb, to rehearse a scene or play. As a noun, the duration of a play's entire performance schedule.

scenery. The onstage pieces of art and architecture designed to create the setting and set of a play.

scenic features. The background and foreground pieces that make up the set. (Figs. 23, 24, 25, 26)

script. The written document describing the actions, words and technical cues comprising the play.

screen. A series of flats, often with scenery painted on both sides, used as a scenic feature or set piece. (Fig. 25)

scrim. A transparent, sheer cloth that, when lighted from the front, shows the audience the painted scene depicted on the front of the scrim; when lighted from the rear, the set (or people) behind the scrim will appear; also called *gauze*.

setting. The description at the beginning of the script that describes where and when a play takes place.

set. As a noun, the space onstage where actors and scenery, and props combine to create the specific world of the play. As a verb, set describes the placing of actors or props in their correct locations before beginning a scene or play.

set piece. A piece of scenery that suggests the environment of the play.

set plan. A diagram that shows where set pieces, scenery and props are situated on stage. (Figs. 29, 30)

snatch basket. A basket or box the stage manager or prop master uses to collect and store hand props.

sound cue chart. A chart made and kept by the sound director that tells exactly what sound cues and effects are needed and when. (Fig. 38)

sound director. The person who operates the sound system and creates sound effects.

sound effect. An artificially produced, often prerecorded sound (usually offstage) that simulates the same sound as it might really occur outside the theatre — gunshots, galloping horses, thunderstorms, etc.

spike. To mark on the stage floor the position of actors, props, and set pieces.

spirit gum. An adhesive substance used to apply beards, mustaches, hair and other items to the face, skin, and head.

spotlight. A light that throws a focused beam onto a small area.

stage. The space where a play is performed. (Figs. 8–13)

stage areas. The nine areas in which the stage is divided for orientation purposes, named from the viewpoint of the actor standing onstage facing the audience — upstage right, upstage center, upstage left, center stage right, center stage, center stage left, downstage right, downstage center, downstage left. (Fig. 2)

stage crew. The persons who handle the technical aspects of putting on the play.

stage directions. The directions in a script that describe the play or scene's time and place, interior or exterior setting, basic information about the characters (their genders, ages, occupations, appearance, mental state), and tell actors when they enter and leave the stage, where actors are supposed to be on the stage, how they move and how they say their lines with what movement, gesture, and facial expressions.

stage manager. The person in charge of making sure everyone on the stage crew has done their job.

stage movements. The stage directions that connote actors' movements around the stage, such as entering, exiting, crossing, turning, kneeling, sitting, rising.

striplights. Lights that are set in a metal trough and generally hung or set along the edge of the stage — footlights, border lights, backing lights, and horizon lights.

strike. The removal by cast and crew of all the scenery, props, costumes, and equipment following the play's final performance.

switchboard. The control device that regulates the lighting cues.

tech table. The table set up to the side or in the back where light and sound operators sit and operate light and sound equipment. (see **booth**)

technical director. The person who brings together all the pieces of the set, which may mean building and painting scenery, constructing the stage, gathering furniture, assembling lighting, and sound equipment.

technical rehearsal. The rehearsal when backstage meets onstage — lighting, sound, and scenery movement are integrated into the total production and any technical problems in these areas are solved.

three-dimensional scenery. A type of scenery that closely replicates a scenic feature in full three-dimensional detail.

thrust stage. A type of stage that has the audience seated on three sides of the acting area, with a part of the stage called the apron extending beyond where the front edge of the stage would normally be. (Fig. 9)

time call. The calls at certain intervals a stage manager gives to actors and crew before a performance: 30 minutes, 15 minutes, 5 minutes, "places!".

tree. The floor stand and pole upon which stage lights are hung. (Fig. 34)

understudy. The actor who has studied a lead actor's part and can take the part if the lead actor is ill or absent.

unit set. One set that is used for all the scenes in the play.

ushers. The persons who assist the house manager in showing the audience to their seats, handing out programs, and maintaining order during the play.

wagon stage. A type of stage on wheels that can serve as an instant stage or be moved onto an existing stage or be moved around the room. (Fig. 12)

walk-through. A rehearsal in which actors proceed slowly through the script, pausing frequently to concentrate on blocking and character interpretation.

wings. The side entrances to the stage that are out of the audience's sight and hidden by a flat or drape; sometimes *the wings* refers to the entire offstage area. (Fig. 8)

— BIBLIOGRAPHY —

Here, in no particular order of precedence or topic, are some books you might find useful in writing and/or presenting your plays with kids.

Hot Tips for Cold Readings: Some Do's and Don'ts for Actors at Auditions by Nina Finburgh. Lyme, N.H.: Smith & Kraus, 1993.

Elegantly Frugal Costumes by Shirley Dearing. Colorado Springs, Colo.: Meriwether Publishers, 1992.

Historic Costumes for the Stage by Lucy Barton. Boston: Walter Baker Company, 1963. Shows 609 pages of incredibly detailed historical costuming from ancient times to the present.

Moving Is Relating: Developing Interpersonal Skills through Movement, Grades 3–6 by Helen Landalf. Lyme, N.H.: Smith & Kraus, 1997.

Patterns for Theatrical Costumes: Garments, Trims, and Accessories from Ancient Egypt to 1915 by Katherine Strand Holkeboer. New York: Drama Book Publishers, 1993.

Stage Management: A Gentle Art by Daniel Bond. New York: Theatre Arts Books, New York, 1992.

Stagecraft 1: A Complete Guide to Backstage Work by William H. Lord. Indianapolis, Ind: William H. Lord, 1991. (9210 N. College)

Dramatizing Mother Goose: The Teacher's Guide to Play Acting in the Classroom, Preschool–Grade 2 by Louise Thistle. Lyme, N.H.: Smith & Kraus, 1997.

The Complete Play Production Handbook by Carl Allensworth. New York: Harper & Row, 1982.

The Smith & Kraus Play Index for Young Actors, Grades K–12 by Craig Slaight and Jennifer Esty. Lyme, N.H.: Smith & Kraus, 1997.

Readers Theatre Fundamentals by Fran Averett Tanner. Topeka, Kans.: Clark Publishing, 1993.

Great Scenes and Monologues for Children by Craig Slaight and Jack Sharrar. Lyme, N.H.: Smith & Kraus, 1993.

Playwriting: The First Workshop by Kathleen E. George. Newton, Mass.: Butterworth-Heinemann, 1994.

The Staging Handbook by Francis Reid. London, England: A & C Black, 1995.

Loving to Audition: The Audition Workbook for Young Actors by Larry Silverberg. Lyme, N.H.: Smith & Kraus, 1996.

Theatre Procedures and Practice, or, Who Does What in the Theatre by Pauline Stuart. Banbury, England: Kemble Press, 1983.

The Theatre of Aurand Harris by Lowell Swortzell. New Orleans, La.: Anchorage Press, 1996. Introduction to the work and theory of a pioneer in children's playwriting.

Dramatics for Children by Eleanor Silverman. Metuchen, N.J.: Scarecrow Press, 1983.

Junior Broadway: How to Produce Musicals with Children by Beverly Ross. Jefferson, N.C.: McFarland Press, 1983.

History of the Theatre by Oscar Brockett. Boston: Allyn & Bacon, 1995.

The Essential Theatre by Oscar Brockett. Ft. Worth, Tex.: Harcourt Brace, 1996.

Practical Drama Handbook by Rosemary Linnell. London, England: Hodder & Stoughton, 1988.

Rehearsing the Audience: Ways to Develop Student Perceptions of Theatre by Ken Davis. Urbana, Ill.: Clearinghouse on Reading & Communication, 1988.

Backwards and Forwards: A Technical Manual for Reading Plays by David Ball. Carbondale, Ill.: Southern Illinois University Press, 1983.

Writing Plays for Young Audiences by Dorothy Webb. Indianapolis, Ind.: Indiana University-Purdue University at Indianapolis, 1996. A video instruction series from Dr. Webb's university class.

Backstage Handbook: An Illustrated Almanac of Technical Information by Paul Carter. New York: Broadway Press, 1994.

Drawings for the Theatre by Robert Edmond Jones. New York: Theatre Arts Books, 1970. Robert Edmond Jones was one of the early twentieth century's pioneers in set design.

The Dramatic Imagination: Reflections and Speculations on the Art of the Theatre by Robert Edmond Jones. New York: Theatre Arts Books, 1973.

Towards a New Theatre: The Lectures of Robert Edmond Jones by Delbert Unruh. New York: Limelight Editions, 1992.

Stage Lighting Revealed: A Design and Execution Handbook by Glen Cunningham. Cincinnati, Ohio: Betterway Books, 1993.

Theatrical Design and Production: An Introduction to Scene Design and Construction, Lighting, Sound, Costume and Makeup by J. Michael Gillette. Mountain View, Calif.: Mayfield Publishing, 1997.

Handbook of Scenery, Properties and Lighting by Harvey Sweet. Boston: Allyn & Bacon, 1995.

The Theater Props Handbook: A Comprehensive Guide to Theater Properties, Materials and Construction by Thurston James. Cincinnati, Ohio: Betterway Books, 1987.

Basic Techniques for Costume Construction by M.L. Baker. Leucadia, Calif.: Theatre Arts Video Library, 1993. Three-video series.

The Face Is a Canvas: The Design and Technique of Theatrical Makeup by Irene Corey. New Orleans, La.: Anchorage Press, 1990.

Stage Rigging Handbook by Jay O. Glerum. Carbondale, Ill.: Southern Illinois University Press, 1997.

Handbook for Sound Engineers: The New Audio Cyclopedia by Glenn Ballou. Indianapolis, Ind.: H.W. Sams, 1987.

Stage Sound by David Collinson. London, England: Cassell, 1982.

Creative Drama in the Primary Grades: A Handbook for Teachers by Nellie McCaslin. Studio City, Calif.: Players Press, 1997.

Multicultural Plays for Children Grades K–3 and Multicultural Plays for Children Grades 4–6 by Pamela Gerke. Lyme, N.H.: Smith and Kraus, 1996.

Stagecrafters' Handbook: A Guide for Theatre Technicians by I.E. Clark. Schulenberg, Tex.: I.E. Clark, 1977.

How to Run a Small Box Office by Kirsten Beck. New York: Off-Off-Broadway Alliance, 1980.

Sing, Anyone Can! by Marci Lynne. Austin, Tex: 1998 (80 Red River Street, Suite #114, Austin, TX 78701-4231). An excellent instructional audio cassette for beginning singers.

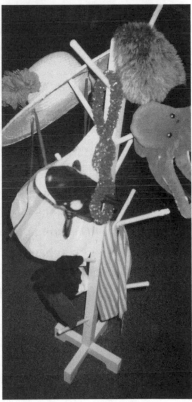

The Author

L.E. McCULLOUGH, PH.D. is a playwright, composer, and ethnomusicologist whose studies in music and folklore have spanned cultures throughout the world. Formerly Assistant Director of the Indiana University School of Music at Indianapolis and a touring artist with Young Audiences, Inc., Dr. McCullough is the Administrative Director of the Humanities Theatre Group at Indiana University-Purdue University at Indianapolis. Winner of the 1995 Playwrights' Preview Productions Emerging Playwright Award for his stage play *Blues for Miss Buttercup*, he is the author of *The Complete Irish Tinwhistle Tutor*, *Favorite Irish Session Tunes*, and *St. Patrick Was a Cajun*, three highly acclaimed music instruction books, and has performed on the soundtracks for the PBS specials *The West* and *Lewis and Clark*. Since 1991 Dr. McCullough has received 35 awards in 26 national literary competitions and had 178 poem and short story publications in 90 North American literary journals. He is a member of The Dramatists Guild, American Conference for Irish Studies, Southeastern Theatre Conference, and National Middle School Association. His books for Smith and Kraus include: *Plays of the Songs of Christmas*, *Stories of the Songs of Christmas*, *Ice Babies in Oz* (character monologues), *Plays of America from American Folklore, Vol. I & II*, *Plays of the Wild West, Vol. I & II*, *Plays from Fairy Tales* and *Plays from Mythology*.